Sixty-Seconds to Yes!©

A Power Method to Mastering Sales & Influence

Don Spini

"America's Top Sales Trainer"

Dedication

To my wife Jessi who is as beautiful on the inside as she is on the outside. Her love and support allowed me to build my own dream. To my beautiful children Katie and Olivia who are the pillars of that dream

Publisher: Motivational Press Inc.
7668 El Camino Real, #104-223
Carlsbad, CA 92009
www.MotivationalPress.com

For Information about custom editions, special sales, premium and corporate purchases, please contact Motivational Press Special Sales Department at 888-357-4441

Table of Contents

Acknowledgments

Many thanks to the following people who have had a positive and generous impact on my life and great input and insight for this book:

Chris Pierson (CFO in Flip Flops), Jacquie Pierson-super chef, John Simmons the Legal Genius, Dave Kemper-Mentor and dear friend, Nichole Kemper, Worth Houghton, Bob Davies, Robin & Dave Muck, Mitch Gaylord our Gold Medal Powerhouse, Rod & Jeri Walz, Courtland Warren, Jake Petrykowski (CEO in Flip Flops), Derek Sabor, Bobby McMullen, Vince Reyes, Jeff Ochoa, Edward Dabran, Lynne Reisinger, Lisa Capper, Teresa Baltao, Sledge, Justin Sachs, , All those in the June 2009 class, Papaw for being there for Olivia at a critical time for us, all the Johnson clan, Nana Judy and Don, Mom for being a great mom and Dad for being a great dad and to my brother's family and sister's family for being patient over the years.

Preface

In the past 25 years in business I have been through massive amounts of sales training. I engaged in them mostly because I believe in constantly improving myself; it is growth or decay, nothing remains static. I did learn things of value from all of training sessions but they all had one glaring problem in common; all they did was try to teach a high-level sales professional how to sell a large piece of equipment to a senior-level executive. There is nothing wrong with this except 99% of the population doesn't engage in that type of encounter. In other words it was just sales training. It went against the natural flow of how people buy!

Each program was riddled in some new questioning method designed to back a potential client into the sales professionals' solution. Words like "funnel" and "probe" were thrown around like a ragdoll.

There was also a race to see who could put the largest binder together with as many "fill-in-the-blank" exercises as they could jam into them. I know because I have a desk full of these binders, covered in dust and many with the blanks still blank!

The instructors were all good people but would ask a series of obvious "self-discovery" questions which (to me) came across as talking down to the audience or filling an arbitrary time commitment.

I learned a little from all but for the most part nothing stuck with me. Maybe it was just me but it seemed my co-workers and business partners felt the same way.

My first ten years in sales I was a failure. I studied the best sales techniques and studied the top sales people in my industry, but nothing gelled. I then realized I was studying the wrong things and the wrong people! I needed to study the *Buyers*! More on that later.

Still I had to ask myself and the sales world some questions; where was the training on how to interview and influence the boss so I was the only one they remember? Where was the training on influencing the loan officer to take a little more risk? Where was the training on influencing your teenager to prevent her from going to summer school if the grades didn't improve? Where was the training on influencing employees to do better and have your boss motivated to listen and implement your ideas? Where was the training on getting your spouse to think a different way and take the Alaskan cruise instead of the tropical vacation and have them thank you for it?

Why does sales training need to be so complicated? Buying or agreeing with a product, service or idea is a natural part of the human condition. Why the need to "trick" people into a decision?

How can we get someone to say "yes" to our product, service or idea in the first few seconds of an engagement, before we ever talk about our product, service or idea?

The previous paragraph is where the book title was developed. You **can** get someone to agree with you up-front and have them ready to buy in seconds. You will discover powerful tools in the first part of the book that do just that.

Here is the other side of the coin; getting the "yes" in a few seconds doesn't mean it will stick until then end...you need to keep the interest high and hold onto the sale until the end; that is critical!

Mastering these types of engagements do not require a top sales professional. They require someone who is **influential**. Influence is 24/7, not just when we are in front of a person trying to buy a product or service.

Selling just happens to be one of the many activities whereby the skill of influence is helpful. To be truly successful we need to be influential in all aspects of life and do so all the time.

Influence is the pillar of strong leadership and a strong relationship. We will develop the meaning of influence as it pertains to this book in chapter two, but know that the most powerful people in the world are skilled purveyors of influence.

What we are going to develop in this book is the skill of influence. Embrace the methodology and you will see dramatic results in your life.

Chapter One

How to Use This Book

This is a fast read and a work book. I don't sugar-coat or add filler and fluff. My goal is to get you the information quickly and succinctly so you can start using it today to be more successful. If I train people on being efficient with words then I need to practice it here. That being said let me give you tips and tools for getting the most out of this workbook.

First, you will notice many words in *italics*. These are definitions used in this book from my individual and corporate training program. I put these terms in *italics* so you will become accustomed to them and start incorporating them into your vocabulary. It is important to start speaking a certain language when dealing with powerful tools of influence; putting names to things you may already do (or are at least aware of) makes them tangible and more real. If you make these terms real you are more likely to use them towards your success!

This is your book, so write in it. There are several places where I guide you to write but don't stop there; highlight and take notes on the pages. If it is written it is real. Make this experience real for you.

The book will follow a sales professional as she guides a client through a selling situation. At the end of each chapter we will add to the scenario the new tools discussed, showing you how the whole process should look. In the example we use a very sterile presentation so you can see it working in a simple form. It is contrite and corny, but that is so you do not get caught up in a drama but rather pay attention to how the tools are being used in the example.

The program is designed to fit your personality. It doesn't train you to say certain things in a certain way. This program does train you on the methodology of influence. Communication & influence is all about the person you are trying to influence, not you. If you have a structure and a plan, it aides your confidence but doesn't change who you are (not canned presentations). Planned conversations work because they give you a level of confidence which allows you to focus on someone else besides yourself.

Influence is a skill. Skills are developed with proper practice over a period of time. You will not read this book and be able to wave a magic wand and have the ability to influence everyone to your way of thinking right away.

You will experience three steps towards developing the skills of selling and influence. The first step is the awkward phase. Picture a baby learning to walk; with proper practice you will migrate from the awkward stage to the mechanical stage. Mechanical means you can do it but it is not transparent and you are thinking too much about what you are doing, making your "influence" noticeable to others. Lastly you will become **natural**. You no longer have to think about what you are doing and can focus purely on the person you are trying to influence. Real influence is the goal and may only be achieved through practice.

Influence is an **advanced communication skill**. Reading, writing, listening and speaking are basic communication skills. You are most likely a natural at these basic skills and you need to know that influence can become just as natural in the same way. Proper practice, small successes and constant feedback are needed for a skill to become natural. Seriously sit in front of a mirror and practice the eight power tools described in this book. It is necessary and will pay immense dividends.

Keep a journal of your experiences while developing these eight *Power Tools*. Refer to it often; you need to mark progress or you will quickly become frustrated. Since I nor my team of instructors and consultants are not there personally to coach and give you feedback you need to do this yourself. It can and will be equally effective if done correctly!

Skills diminish if not used. Let me repeat: Skills diminish if not used. You probably spoke Spanish fairly well in high school but today that language is a mystery once again. If you don't use these skills daily they will weaken and eventually disappear. You need to ask yourself, when will I be done being a leader? When will I be done building a wealth legacy for my family? When will I no longer want to make peoples' lives better? If this is true why then would you not constantly work on improving your skills of influence? These skills of influence are there for the good of all human-kind. As a sincere influential person, they are there for the effective communication in your personal and professional life. Use these tools for good or lose them, it is that simple.

Chapter Two

Introduction to Mastering Influence

Your success should be a byproduct of the good you do for others, not the reason for the good you do for others.

A few years ago my wife was offered a great business opportunity in San Diego, California. At the time we lived in Orange County, California and both worked in Orange County. Since this was a great opportunity and knowing we could tough out a commute we decided to split the difference of the 70-mile stretch and find something between Orange County and San Diego.

This was our first move together so we need to explore each other's preferences. My wife is a country girl. She was raised on a farm in the mid-west. She loves nature, wide-open spaces and the privacy the country brings.

I am a city/beach kind of a guy. I like being close to the action; restaurants, entertainment, shopping, you name it.

So, my wife loves the country and I love the city. When it came time to find our new home between San Diego and Orange County we had to compromise. So guess where we moved?

The country.

My wife and I love animals. My wife wanted three German Shepherds from the local rescue and I wanted one good German Shepherd from the local rescue. We decided to compromise. Guess how many dogs we have?

Four.

I have a passion for nice cars. My wife has no love for nice cars. When it was time for a new car I wanted the top-of-the-line something. Now that we had all this country land and dogs my wife thought we might consider a nice truck. No way. I would never be caught dead in a truck. We decided to compromise. Guess what I drive.

A truck.

I know what the guys reading this are thinking and I will say you are wrong (most likely).

The fact is my wife is **very influential** in my life. Let me explain. My wife was able to get me to think a different way. She was able to get me to **change my mind** about what I thought I wanted. That by itself doesn't make her influential. Here is what makes her influential; **I love the decisions she has helped me make!** By that I mean this; I absolutely love my home in the country. I didn't know how or if it was for me but now I wouldn't leave that house for anything. I love the privacy, land and the natural way of life as much as she does.

I love those dogs. I never thought I would want more than one dog but these dogs have given our family three important gifts: gratitude for saving them, companionship unlike anything most humans can procure and a very important level of security for our home that no alarm or security guard could ever provide. I am 100% comfortable traveling away from home knowing that there are four German Shepherds sleeping at the foot of our stairs protecting my family with their lives.

I will always have a truck. That truck has paid for itself on the ranch ten-fold since we bought it. Everyone needs a truck (nothing more zealous than a convert, huh??). Don't get me wrong, I still like nice cars but will always have a truck.

You see, my wife was able to change my mind and have it be better for me than the direction I was thinking. **That is the essence of influence my friends!**

Influence is getting someone to change their mind and agree with you and have that decision be better for them. They will thank you for helping them see a better way! Influence fosters what we know as the *Win/Win*.

Let's look at manipulation. Manipulation is where you get me to change my mind and it is good for you but bad for me. We know this as *Win/Lose*.

Here is a big "Did-You-Know"; **the tools and skills used to influence are the same tools and skills used to manipulate!** Repeat; the tools and skills used to influence are the same tools and skills used to manipulate!

The true and only difference between influence and manipulation is **your intention.**

Here is a simple example. If I were a carpenter (skill) I could take a hammer (tool) and use my skills to build a home for Habitat for Humanity and give a homeless person a new house. I can also take my skills and the hammer (tool) to hit you on the head and steal your wallet or purse. It is the same skill and tool, but my intentions create an entirely different outcome.

Point: Use the powerful tools in the book for influence, not manipulation. The return will be a thousand fold and you'll be the person you want to be.

My eight *Power Tools* are skills to master communication and influence, having *Win/Win* encounters in business and personal relationships. In other words, *Win/Win* in life.

To summarize, influence is *Win/Win* and manipulation is *Win/Lose*.

Another "Did-You-Know"; did you know manipulation is not the worst outcome? There is another scenario which generates the saddest and sometimes the most devastating result; *Lose/Lose*. *Lose/Lose* occurs when you have a product, service or idea that you know will make a positive and valuable difference in someone's life and <u>you cannot influence them to take action</u>. You cannot convince them and as a result they do not reap the benefits you propose.

What is the price they pay? What is the price you pay? What about their family? Your family? Society? You see, to influence is to <u>always</u> make the world a better place. If true, then there has to be an opposite. We owe it to ourselves, family, friends and society to do all we can to help others.

Note: For those of you keeping score I was able to draw the line with my wife regarding cats. No cats, period. I have nothing against cats or cat lovers I just don't like cats as pets. So we compromised.

We have only two cats.

Which by the way live in the master bedroom and spend their time sleeping on my chest and blowing dander up my allergy-prone nostrils. That, my friends, is manipulation! Moving on...

Chapter Three

Three Types of Communication Encounters

Let us start with basic knowledge about communication that by itself will make you more aware and thus more successful.

Did you know that there are only three types of *Communication Encounters*? (Italic alert...a definition). In your interactions with other humans only three things are happening when you engage one another from a communication perspective. It is important to know and identify these because there are different degrees as to how we can influence others based on what kind of encounter we are experiencing.

The first type of *Communication Encounter* is what we identify as *Casual Conversation*. This is usually you talking about you and someone else talking about them. This is low-yield from a success and influence perspective but high-yield from a social perspective. In short, there is little to gain here in the form of influencing others. If I had to give you any advice (in regards to *Casual Conversation*), I would say let others talk 90% of the time and ask them questions about them. **It is everyones' favorite topic**.

The second type of *Communication Encounter* is *Exchange of Information and Direction*. In this encounter you get information, you give information, you get direction and you give direction. *Exchange of Information and Direction* has a much higher yield for our success in influencing because this is where the control component begins. When you give information or direction, you are in control of the encounter. Control is crucial to influence.

During the *Exchange of Information & Direction* encounter, it is critical to recognize we have the opportunity to qualify the *Buyer* (another italic word). If you have ever been involved in any sales training you have been told to do the qualifying of the *Buyer* in the questioning portion of your sales event, but we train on a different philosophy.

In our program we train our participants not to waste valuable **influence** time asking for basic information. If you are looking for information about how qualified the *Buyer* is then you are in *Exchange of Information and Direction.* Save your influence time on influencing!

Are you ready for the **Grand Daddy** of all communication encounters? Welcome to your single-greatest opportunity to sell and influence others. We call this *Communication Encounter* the **Buy-Sell-Encounter**!

This powerful encounter is at the **heart of influence**. Let me be clear, this is not simply when we are selling a product or service for monetary gain. We as humans are in *Buy-Sell-Encounters* every day, several times a day. The question is do you know you are in it and **do you know how to win it**? When I say you need to be influential in all aspects I mean you need to know how to recognize *Buy-Sell-Encounters* and know how to win them in all situations.

Some examples of *Buy-Sell-Encounters* are trying to influence your spouse to try a different restaurant or go to another movie, talking to a loan officer at the bank or motivating your employees to do a better job. These are all *Buy-Sell-Encounters* that will effect your success and leadership abilities in all areas of your life.

Here is the definition of a *Buy-Sell-Encounter* as described in this program:

There is a *Buyer*...there is a *Seller*...and the key component making it a true *Buy-Sell-Encounter* is this; a **decision is made every...single...time!** Here's how it looks graphically:

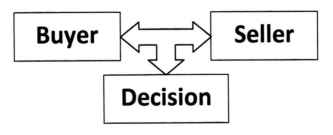

Buy-Sell-Encounter™

If someone is asking you to make a decision, you are the *Buyer*. If you are asking someone to make a decision you are the *Seller*. We use these terms as standard throughout the book.

If you as a *Seller* ask for a decision and it comes back favorable for you <u>and the *Buyer*</u>, you leave the *Buy-Sell-Encounter* as the *Seller* influencing a *Win/Win* from the event. Conversely, if you as a Seller ask for a decision and it comes back favorable for you and unfavorable for the Buyer, you leave the *Buy-Sell-Encounter* as the *Seller* manipulating a *Win/Lose* from the event. A important point to remember is the same tools and skills used to influence are the same skills and tools used to manipulate, it is the Sellers intention that matters. Manipulation isn't the worst thing that can happen in a *Buy-Sell-Encounter*. If you have a product, service or idea that will benefit the Buyer and you can't get them to buy, you leave the *Buy-*

Sell-Encounter with a Lose/*Lose* from the event. The Buyer loses, the Seller loses, both families lose, society loses, at least with manipulation some one benefited. However, it isn't right and we focus on using the Power Tools to create Win/Win in the *Buy-Sell-Encounter.*

You bought the objection or the "no". Don't worry; it happens to all of us. The question is can you dramatically increase the wins and decrease the losses? The answer is a resounding YES!

The more wins you string together in **all areas of your life** the more success you will experience and pass along to others.

This book is your blue print for winning the *Buy-Sell-Encounter.* It is the primary function of my training program. There is a simple, conscious methodology that we teach and an intentional direction you will take to master the *Buy-Sell-Encounter.*

To summarize there are only three types of *Communication Encounters:*

Casual Conversation – Low yield for influence; possible high-yield socially.

Exchange of Information and Direction – *Higher* yield, as this encounter allows us develop our power of control and qualify the *Buyer.*

The Buy-Sell-Encounter –Our greatest opportunity to influence. **You need to know you are in it and how to win it!**

Let's get going!

22

Chapter Four

The Decision Process

Let us start this chapter with another big "Did-You-Know" statement. Assuming you are in an *Exchange of Information and Direction* or a *Buy-Sell-Encounter*, let's talk about how decisions are made. Did you know that everyone living human on the planet makes decisions the **exact same way**!

We do and I will spend a good part of this chapter proving this. I have cleverly named this phenomenon *The Decision Process*. We identify *The Decision Process* as a three-step process. It has a beginning, middle and an end. Influential *Sellers* know this process and can effectively navigate *Buyers* through this process towards a successful outcome.

Each of these three areas are specifically addressed in this book and are crucial for you to understand if you are going to be effective in influencing *Buyers* through the process.

Let us break down the three steps of *The Decision Process* and what the *Buyer* goes through while in each area.

Phase One of *The Decision Process- Exploration*

The first phase of *The Decision Process* is the *Exploration* phase. Here the *Buyer* starts by making an **emotional connection** to a product, service or idea. I call it the *Exploration* phase because we explore the possibility of buying whatever has caught our interest. We start by saying to our self "I need" or "I want" something. Satisfying a need or a want is an emotional process.

NOTE: Get the highlighter out because what I say next is very, very, **VERY** important: **If the** *Buyer* **doesn't make a strong emotional connection to your product, service or idea there is very little chance of them buying.** You as the *Seller* need to know this because it may be the single most important statement in the entire book.

I will add it does not matter how boring, sterile or bland the product, service or idea; the decision to move forward is based purely on emotion.

People buy everything based on emotion. Repeat. People buy everything based on emotion. **The decision process starts in the heart!**

Getting the *Buyer* to make a strong emotional connection to you and your product, service or idea is accomplished by the *Seller* continuing to raise the *Level of Interest* throughout the *Exploration* phase of The *Decision Process*. We will train you on a four-step process dedicating four of eight *Power Tools* to accomplish this most important task.

It is important to note this is where people struggle with our process. I want you to read the following section as many times needed until you fully believe the concept because it is 100% true and if you fail to understand it, you will never get there with my methodology.

If we believe (and we do) people buy on emotion and the first part of the *Decision Process* is the emotional portion, then it is a logical conclusion that the decision to buy is made in the very beginning of the *Decision Process*, not at the end when the *Seller* asks for the business. Let me emphasize this point; the decision to buy the product, service or idea is made in the **very beginning** of the *Buy-Sell-Encounter*.

Did you get that? *Sellers* have been taught by other programs that decisions are made after *Buyers* examine all the information. This is not accurate. Now, let me be clear, the decision to buy is made early in the emotional phase but **it does not mean it is going to stick**! A lot can and does happen to undo that decision. Most often it is undone by the *Seller* through bad sales presentations and poor influence skills.

Important: The *Seller's* purpose in the *Exploration* phase is to elevate the *Level of Interest* of the *Buyer* to a level that gets them to say "yes" to the product, service or idea before the *Seller* ever presents or talks about their product, service or idea! If this doesn't make sense now it will shortly. Hang in there!

This program will help you develop that skill via a four-step process for elevating the *Level of Interest* in the *Buyer* causing the *Buyer* to say "please show me how you can do this for me!" Chapters 5, 6, 7 & 8 will address these four steps with four *Power Tools* to successfully navigate the *Exploration* phase.

We buy on emotion and we validate with logic.

Phase Two of *the Decision Process – Validation*

Once we make the decision to buy based on a strong emotional connection (heart), as *Buyers* we seek out proof, facts and evidence to *Validate* the decision as a good one (head/brain). As we move to the middle of *The Decision Process;* the *Validation* phase, it is important to note that it is here where the *Seller* is most likely to lose the favorable decision. The reason is simple; the *Seller* gets to talk about himself or herself. Here comes the big presentation the *Seller* has practiced over and over!

Throughout the entire *Exploration* phase all the *Seller* did was focus on the *Buyer*. Now it is his/her turn and the *Seller*'s *Credibility Curve* is about to take a downturn. There are two reasons for loss of credibility.

The first is natural and can be mitigated easily. We lose some credibility whenever we move the focus from the *Buyer* to us as a *Seller*. This is normal and not a big deal. Everyones' favorite conversational subject is <u>them</u>, therefore when we take the focus away from them (although briefly) their interest will begin to drop.

It is the second reason that really can sink the ship. Here is another big "Did-You-Know". Did you know in a *Buy-Sell-Encounter* you get accused of lying even when you are telling the truth? Your credibility is shot and your chances of winning the encounter are greatly diminished when a *Buyer* thinks you are lying (not exactly an epiphany statement, I know).

Remember I said you are accused of lying even though you were not. How is this possible? Simple, *Sellers* do not fully understand the difference between a *Fact* and a *Claim*. I see this over and over when working with top sales professionals – I am talking about the good ones and they still struggle with this concept.

Let me be clear, when you know you are lying and you get caught that is your problem. What about when you are telling the truth but the *Buyer* does not believe you?

Simple, the *Buyer* thinks you are giving them *Claims*, not *Facts*.

Folks, a *Claim* is not necessarily a lie. A *Claim* can be 100% true but the *Buyer* does not believe it at **face** value. The *Seller* knows it to be true but it is not about what she believes. Because the Seller states it and knows it is a fact is not enough. The *Seller* needs to show sufficient proof and evidence, in a proper and powerful manner to back up the *Claim* and turn it into a *Fact* **in the *Buyers* mind**! We have two *Power Tools* in chapters 9 & 10 to show you how to do this and mitigate the *Credibility Curve* downturn.

Remember, the decision to buy was already made in the *Exploration* phase, make it stick. Do not screw it up in the *Validation* phase.

Phase Three of the Decision Process – Resolution

Here is another big "Did-You-Know" statement. Did you know that **there are objections to every single decision made**? I have to say that in my experience the vast majority of sales professionals have no idea this is true.

Sales professionals in general hate objections. The reason is simply that they are not comfortable or confident in overcoming them. Sales professionals hate objections for the same reason I hate golf – when you are bad at something you tend not to like it very much!

Fear not my friends because I am about to let you in on a secret; objections are a natural part of *The Decision Process*. Buyers always go through what I identify as the third phase or *Conflict Resolution*. We need to resolve conflict (decision moves from our head to our gut), outstanding issues and concerns before we make our final decision to move forward. I said it is part of the natural progression, therefore nothing to fear.

That being said, so many people are afraid and hindered by objections. Let us break it down and take the mystery and fear away by starting with some basic knowledge.

A big "Did-You-Know" is there are only **four** objections in the entire world. If you have been in sales a while you probably think you have heard at least 16,586 different objections but in fact that they all fit into four buckets.

Here they are (drum roll please)...

- ✓ **Time**

- ✓ **Money**

- ✓ **Lack of Need/Want/Desire**

...and the Mother-of-All-Objections...

- ✓ *Fear of Change!!*

That is it. Only four. By the way that last one is a **BIG DEAL**. Do not underestimate it. More on that later.

Here are some important points to remember as we navigate through *Conflict Resolution*:

- ✓ People sometimes lie (shocking, I know); not always out of malice. They do not always tell you the real objection out of fear. They will say it is time or money but how do you know they are telling the truth?

- ✓ The likely real and <u>only</u> objection is *Fear of Change*.

- ✓ Never underestimate the power the *Fear of Change* has on the *Buyers'* inability to make a decision.

- ✓ **People resent & resist change, even when it is good for them**!! (Read this 1,000 times, seriously)

- ✓ The greater the decision, the greater the *Fear of Change*.

IMPORTANT POINT: By definition when you are influencing someone you are asking them to **make a change. If people naturally resist change can you see why you are having a problem getting them to say yes?**

There are two components to handling objections: first you must find the real objection and second you need to handle it with confidence. Easier said than done, I know. We have two power tools to successfully navigate the *Buyer* through *Conflict Resolution* which you will discover in chapters 11 and 12. They show you how to do the two things previously mentioned; find the real objection and then how to overcome the objection with grace, ease and most importantly, confidence. These tools are only part of the equation. There is more to handling *Conflict Resolution* and overcoming objections than these tools alone.

Let me cover some of the details you will need to know to help you better position yourself prior to overcoming objections. Here is an analogy to set up the attitude you need to have when going into the *Resolution* phase:

If you can, picture in your mind a fighter jet about to land on an aircraft carrier. You look underneath the plane and see a long piece of metal with a curved end hanging down near the back of the aircraft. That is the tail hook. On the deck of the aircraft carrier you see there are three cables lying perpendicular across the deck. These cables are called arresting wires. The ideal situation is the plane touches down and the tail hook will catch one of the three cables and brings the aircraft to a very abrupt stop (no kidding, huh?).

Here is the question for you: When the pilot senses his landing gear touch down on the deck of the aircraft carrier, what does he do?

If you said "hit the brakes" you are incorrect. In fact the pilot knows to hit full throttle! Why? If in the chance he misses all three of the arresting wires with the tail hook he has enough power to take off and try again. It happens quite frequently. If the pilot hits the brakes and misses the wires he would not have enough power to take off, instead ending up in the Big Blue Drink.

The pilot is **conditioned** to **expect** to miss all the wires. In fact, he **expects** to take off again. When the wire does catch the tail hook the pilot is actually surprised, even though that is the definition of a successful landing.

How does this analogy apply to you and successful navigation through *Conflict Resolution*? The exact same **attitude** needs to be in your head when you get past *Validation* and into *Resolution*. By that I mean this: You need to **expect** the *Buyer* to have objections to your product, service or idea. You need to **expect** to go deep into *Conflict Resolution* after you ask for the decision or business. Knowing this you also need to have the proper skills to overcome and resolve objections.

What most *Sellers* **expect** after making their case (*Validation*) is the *Buyer* to jump up and down and say "I'll take it!!" When they do not react in the expected way, the wind is knocked out of the *Seller's* sail and they take it as either a personal affront or a rejection of the product, service or idea. People hate rejection! I mean how can the *Buyer* not see the obvious value of what I am selling or proposing??!!

It is not a personal affront or a rejection. The *Buyer* is doing what you and I do naturally whenever we make any decision, resolving conflict. I will beat this statement into the ground but it is very important; dealing with conflict last in *The Decision Process* is a natural progression. You will be able to handle this natural progression with a whole new attitude. Stay with me!

To summarize this chapter let me illustrate what I call the "anatomy of a decision" In other words what actually happened to make them buy or agree with you. Below is the formula and the physiological areas of the body each area affects:

$$\text{Value} \geq \text{Cost=Win}$$

Value must be equal-to or greater than the cost. Two things about this are important to know. First, **value is established in the very beginning of the *Decision Process*** (*Exploration*) by the *Buyer*, not you the *Seller*.

The value of your product, service or idea is established before you ever present your product, service or idea. Interesting concept, huh?

Second, what is cost? Cost is often misunderstood by *Sellers* as the monetary price. **Cost is made up of all four objections combined; time, money, lack of need, want or desire and *Fear of Change*.** In a decision one may stand out more than another, but all four exist to some degree. When someone asks "how much does it cost" and we only address the price tag we are missing 75% of the equation.

If value is not established equal-to or greater than cost it is very tough to get a decision in your favor. The next four chapters are dedicated to showing you how to raise interest to an extreme level, which drives up the value of your product, service or idea **before** you begin talking about your product, service or idea!

Leave this chapter with the formula imbedded in your mind:

A favorable decision (*Win/Win*) is made when *Value* is equal-to or greater than *Cost*!

$$\textit{Value} \geq \textit{Cost} = \textbf{Yes!}$$

Physical Affects of the *Decision Process*

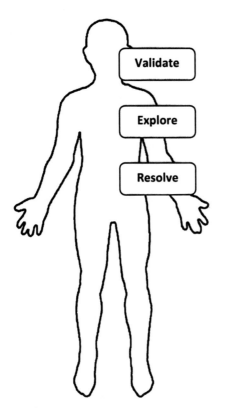

The *Decision Process* moves through physiological places in the body as it progresses, starting with the heart (*Explore*), making the emotional connection then moving to the head (*Validate*)for logic and reason and ending in the gut (*Resolve*) to resolve outstanding issues and conflict.

Chapter Five

Statement of Great Importance (SOGI)

Purpose of The *SOGI* – Remember how I said in the previous chapter the *Buyer* makes the decision to buy up-front, in the beginning of the *Decision Process*? This is because they need to make the emotional connection to buy. Before the *Buyer* can make that emotional connection the *Seller* needs to start the encounter and have the full and complete attention of the *Buyer*. The *SOGI* is designed to do just that; grab the full and complete attention of the *Buyer* and to give the *Seller* a specific entry point for the *Buy-Sell-Encounter*.

Position in the *Decision Process*:

▲ *Statement of Great Importance* – First Step in the *Decision Process* and your first power tool of influence (remember when the *Buyer* actually makes his/her decision.)

It is important for your confidence to know the exact point in time the *Buy-Sell-Encounter* begins and have a tool to ensure a proper control. The *Buyer* doesn't necessarily need to be aware of the official beginning, but you the Seller need to know. Since the *Decision Process* works **in sequence** it makes sense to give you a tool that launches the *Buy-Sell-Encounter* with power. *The SOGI* is that tool.

SOGI is our acronym for *Statement of Great Importance*. Besides marking the beginning of the *Buy-Sell-Encounter*, it serves a very important role in navigating the *Decision Process*; **it helps you to get the *Buyer's* full attention and have them completely focused on you.**

To understand this tool it is important for you to reflect on two crucial points in influencing decisions. First point is this; **you do not matter in the *Decision Process*!** I will add here an important question; do you want to be right or do you want to win the decision?

Do you want to talk about what is important to you or do you want to win the decision? Many times these desires work against each other.

Second, we need to take time to explore an important element in any decision, the difference between **needs** and **wants**.

Here is another important "Did-You-Know" moment:

Did you know every product, service or idea does **two things** and **only** two things for the *Buyer*? Those two things are **prevent bad things and deliver good things**. It does not matter how fun the product, how sterile the service or how complicated the solution or idea is. It is that simple and you need to keep things simple. I am not talking about the features of the product, service or idea I am simply talking about how the human brain works.

The human brain exists for one primary purpose only: Survival. That survival mechanism is designed to steer us away from pain and move us closer towards comfort. You would think such a complicated and sophisticated biological device would have a higher purpose, but it doesn't. Sorry to disappoint. As *Sellers,* understanding the survival mechanism is a critical advantage.

There are two types of people in the world; those that run from pain (my buddy Vince for example) and those that run towards pleasure (me for example). Here is an exercise to calibrate what type of person you may be. Below are five pairs of phrases. Please take a pen and circle the phrase in each pair that has the **most emotional impact** to you. Don't over-think it!

Lose Job – Make More Money

Prevent Losses – Increase Revenue

Stop Losing Employees – Improve Employee Moral

Avoid Illness – Be Healthier

Eliminate Lawsuits – Add More Protection

Do you tend to have a stronger emotional connection the left column (run from pain) or the right column (run towards pleasure)? With the participants in the training program it usually is split right down the middle.

 Here is the point that I do not want you to forget; it does not matter what **you** like or what area is more emotionally charged to you. It is the *Buyer*'s perspective the *Seller* needs to explore. Here is where I interject the **crucial** concept that sets the tone for the entire chapter:

Needs vs. Wants

When I say every product, service or idea stops a bad thing that means addressing the *Need*. When I say every product delivers a good thing that means addressing the *Want*. In the *Decision Process* when you want to influence the decision, you need to make sure **you uncover both the need and the want** for the *Buyer*.

37

When trying to get the *Buyer's* attention, which concept has more emotional connection for him/her? Let me share a story to help you understand the best way to get the *Buyer*'s attention in the first few seconds of the *Decision Process*:

My wife and I did a remodel on our home. 90% of the remodel was for her, 10% for me. The 10% for me was my home theatre, AKA the Man Cave! I love my home theatre and put significant effort into the planning and development. It is a first-class room for any sports or movie fan. Here is a partial list of the equipment:

Full 7.1 surround sound, powered sub-woofer, built-in speaker system, DVD player, surround sound amplifier, huge comfortable couch with chaise lounge and of course the crown jewel of the entire system...the 52 inch flat screen LCD 1080i HD television! The TV is recessed into the wall like a movie screen! Wow!

Just a few days after completing the remodel my wife and I went to a local casino resort to see a show. We had dinner and with time left to kill we wandered around exploring the facility. I noticed they had a poker room and we went inside to check it out. Upon entering something immediately caught my eye that changed my life forever (so I thought at the time).

On the wall of the poker room was a flat screen television. That is not impressive by itself but what was impressive was the size. It was at least <u>eight</u> <u>feet</u> <u>wide</u>! A real commercial flat screen! What is more is the picture was perfect! I swear I heard angels singing in my head as I watched the flawless HD picture unfold before my eyes.

I looked at my wife and said with complete conviction "I WANT THAT TV"! As you would expect she immediately dismissed my idea with a roll of her eyes and a little laughter. She misread the situation and my steel resolve. I was dead serious. I WANT THAT TV! I said no more to my wife that night and we went on to enjoy the show.

I remembered a graduate of my training program sold high-end video equipment so I called him the next day to inquire what something like that would run from a price perspective.

He said that particular TV runs about $25,000. Ouch, conflict resolution. Sure it is a lot of money for a TV, but I could actually afford it if I wanted (according to me, a man...maybe not so much if you ask my wife!). A bit pricey but guess what, I WANT THAT TV!

As of the writing of this book was written I still haven't bought that TV. Why? Simple. I already had a brand new flat screen TV in my home theatre. I *wanted* that other TV, but I did not *need* it. Now, I live in Southern California. If by chance some disaster fell upon my current TV such as a faulty mounting bracket breaking without explanation (wink wink) and Southern California had a small earthquake, it might fall and break into a thousand pieces, I would then *need* a new TV and *I am much more likely to take action* towards a purchase.

Important point: You can *WANT* something forever and never buy it or take action. When you *NEED* something you will more likely take action now!

What we need we need now, what we want we may defer to a later date or never.

Here is what you need to take away from this chapter; if you want to get someone to take immediate action in your favor on your product, service or idea, you need to first get their **full attention** by addressing the **need** your product, service or idea satisfies.

Remember, every product, service or idea satisfies both needs and wants, so we need to start with the one with the strongest emotional connection to truly get the *Buyer*'s attention. This must happen in the first few seconds of the *Buy-Sell-Encounter*. The *Statement of Great Importance* accomplishes this goal.

Practical Application

You've had *Casual Conversation*, you've qualified the *Seller* or gave something of value with *Exchange of Information or Direction*, now it is time to enter the *Buy-Sell-Encounter*.

The Statement of Great Importance defined is a statement or rhetorical question designed to start a *Buy-Sell-Encounter* using needs-based words such as "prevent", "eliminate", "avoid" or "stop" to name a few.

Examples:

"It is important in today's economy not to **lose** your job."

"You most likely need to **avoid** losing clients."

"You don't want to have a **miserable** vacation, right?"

"It is crucial for your business to **prevent** employee turnover."

"You need to **stop** the bleeding."

These samples are directed at stopping bad things. This is sometimes difficult for many people to grasp as it is our nature to want to provide good things. Remember, since all products, services and ideas stop bad things and deliver good things don't worry, you'll get to the good stuff soon enough.

We are trying to make the **strongest emotional connection** as soon as possible so we can enlist a greater desire for a **call to action**. To do this we need to "Hit a Nerve" in the very beginning of the *Buy-Sell-Encounter*. Points to note are the *Buyer* may have no idea yet what product, service or idea you are presenting. That is perfectly ok. People do not buy products, services or ideas, they buy the "what" and the "why" you are going to uncover in the *Exploration* phase.

You are not trying to close them on anything with the *SOGI*, just merely trying to get them to stop thinking about their cell phone or email and focus entirely on you for the moment.

Some guidelines for using *The Statement of Great Importance*:

The more emotional the statement the better.

Make no product, service or idea references in the statement.

It is all about the *Buyer*…avoid using words like "Me", "I", "Our" and "We".

Keep it as short as possible. The less words the more powerful.

Ensure you are "Hitting a Nerve", you have a solution so be direct.

Now, think of a real situation where you need to influence a decision. Write down different approaches using your *SOGI*

What decision (win/win) do I want in this specific *Buy-Sell-Encounter*?

_____

Sample *SOGI*?

1._____

2._____

3._____

Key Point:

Practice the *SOGI* several times so it sounds natural. Practice doesn't make perfect, practice makes permanent! Practice the right way to make this a natural skill.

At the end of each chapter I will develop a role-play scenario so you may see the method being used. The role-play will develop and grow with each chapter so you may see the flow. Let us now start the *Buy-Sell-Encounter*:

Summary Point:

Regardless, if you are planning a formal presentation or a spur-of –the-moment *Buy-Sell-Encounter* take time to prepare a powerful, emotional and needs-based *Statement of Great Importance*. Should I emphasize the point that the *SOGI* should be a *Statement of Great*

Importance to the *Buyer*, not you the *Seller*? Do not forget this. It is all about the *Buyer*!

Chapter Six

The Menu

Purpose of *The Menu* – In the previous chapter we explored the *SOGI* and how to gain the attention of the *Buyer*; the *Menu* ensures the *Seller* actually has a solution for the *Buyer*. The *Menu* will get the *Buyer* conditioned to buy up-front and say "yes" to your product, service or idea before you ever present your product, service or idea! You will also eliminate one of the four objections (from chapter 4) with the *Menu*; Lack of need, want or desire. You will discover this early in the decision process, not at the end!

Position in the *Decision Process*:

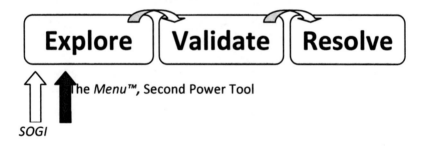

SOGI

We know the decision to buy is made early in the *Decision Process*, specifically in the *Exploration* phase. Sure, a lot can happen to change that decision as the *Buyer* navigates through the *Decision Process,* but nonetheless *Buyers* make a strong emotional connection first and either a) talk ourselves out of it or b) move forward with positive action.

I constantly make the statement in my program that it is important to get the *Buyer* to say "yes" to our product, service or idea **before** we actually talk about or present our product, service or idea. This doesn't make sense to a lot of people as they are under the false impression that talking about themselves, their product, service or idea is how you get people interested in them. You will see this is not true for one very specific reason; it is not human nature. *Buyers* must elevate and maintain interest in whatever decision they are making otherwise they simply do not buy. The *Buyer's* interest lies in their emotional connection, not the *Seller's* product, service or idea.

The *Seller* is charged with the duty of helping the *Buyer* elevate their interest to the highest level early and maintaining it throughout the decision process.

Now time to implement one of the most powerful tools of influence; *The Menu*! Many of my training students point to *The Menu* as one of their favorite power tools in the program. To introduce *The Menu* let us walk through the philosophy behind this powerful methodology.

Please answer the following questions to yourself as you read. Although you may find them rhetorical and overly-simple you really need to answer them as it is material and important to the understanding of *The Menu.*

When you go into a restaurant and are seated by the host or hostess they hand you something. What do the hand you? A menu. Why do they hand you a menu? What specific purposes does it serve? Again, these seemingly obvious questions have a lot of power to them once we explore the answers.

The menu handed you in a restaurant is an extremely useful tool. The menu is a list of choices the restaurant provides. It's what they do and likely do best.

The two powerful functions the menu does are broken down in the following way:

1. If you don't see anything you like on the menu you are free to leave and there is no transaction.

    What is powerful about this concept is the decision not to proceed is made early in the restaurant experience, not at the end when everyone wasted a lot of time and effort. If there is a *lack of need or want* (the only objection we cannot overcome) it is discovered early before time is wasted.

2. Read the following two sentences slowly and carefully so you fully understand the importance. If you select an item on the menu what have you just done? You just bought! You said **yes** in the **very beginning** of the restaurant experience.

    Here is an important point; you do not know if you will like the item yet, you don't know if you'll end up paying for the item yet, you haven't *validated* your decision yet but nonetheless you already **made the decision to buy** in the first 10% of the restaurant (*Decision*) process.

    You just selected an item based on an extreme emotional connection and said "I'll take it". Again, **much can happen to change that decision and it might not stick, but the decision to move forward with action is made early**.

Taking that analogy, let's move to the *Decision Process* and see how a menu may be used to create the same response in the *Buyer* as a menu in the restaurant does for the patron.

To explore this concept let us look at conventional wisdom (which is neither wise nor conventional) when it comes to most selling situations. What we have been told our entire adult lives in regards to selling is we need to ask a lot of questions. True, but not the way we have been taught. You see the questioning methods taught in most programs deal with the word "probing". We need to ask probing questions.

There is a major flaw with probing (besides the word itself! Look it up...no one wants to be probed!). There are two powerful forces at work when we are in the decision process; **Interest** and **Defenses**. These forces work **opposite** of each other. **When one goes up the other goes down!** Our job as a *Seller* is to keep interest moving in an upward direction and keep defenses moving in a downward direction (suppressed).

The problem with "probing" is it inadvertently has the effect of raising defenses and lowering interest. Here is why; the way the *Seller*, skilled or unskilled is asking the questions. Probing questions while on the surface seem like the *Seller* is becoming interested in the *Buyer*, the *Buyer* is experiencing the exact opposite feeling.

Let me explain this phenomenon. In the simplest of terms the *Seller* is asking questions in such a manner as to "funnel" the *Buyer* into a solution that the *Seller* is hiding behind their back.

The *Seller* won't reveal the solution yet until they are sure the *Buyer* (via answering leading and targeted questions) shows a need or want for the hidden solution indirectly through the answers given.

The *Buyer* becomes aware that they are being "funneled" and immediately raise their **defenses**. When defenses go up, positive decisions become more difficult and less likely.

You know exactly what I mean because you have experienced this hundreds if not thousands of times in your life. You and I as *Buyers* will be thinking in our head "Where is this going" when someone is asking us questions but have not really identified why they are asking them! We know they are selling something but our skepticism/defenses start to rise with every leading question.

Specifically the *Seller* has not told us <u>first</u> what is in it for us, hence our defenses go up and our interest goes down.

The question is why hide your solutions and benefits? Imagine if in a restaurant they did not give you a menu first? Wouldn't it be frustrating if you sat down and the waiter asked you a slew of questions before showing you what they have to offer in the menu? You would be frustrated at the experience and be unlikely to make a favorable decision.

What if you walked into an electronics store to buy a TV and there were no TVs on display, instead the store clerk would grill you for 20 minutes about how much you want to spend, what size TV and why you want it etc. You'd be very frustrated.

The same holds true for *The Menu* methodology. You need to present the **benefits** of buying or agreeing with you **up front**, in the very beginning of the decision process! This needs to happen right after the *SOGI* and before you begin your questioning (in our case, our questioning methodology is a much more powerful and effective technique called *The Journey*, taught in the very next chapter).

What specifically is *The Menu*? Before I answer this in practical detail let us participate in an exercise we conduct in our training program.

Let me ask you a question; what is in it for me (the *Buyer*) if I buy/agree with you? Think of a situation where you need someone to buy/agree with you in the near future and then answer the following question by writing your response below (take your time with this one):

By buying/agreeing with me the *Buyer* will benefit because:

_____

Let me walk you through some questions for you to answer in your head.

> 1. Did you come up with only one benefit, yes or no?

This is not necessarily a good thing. One solution does not appeal to everyone. You need to broaden the appeal of your solution by broadening the potential benefits.

For example if your solution will save the *Buyer* money, not everyone will be attracted to that specific benefit. If that is all that is on your *Menu* you are **limiting** the chances of elevating the *Buyer* interest.

I will add this caveat; if you are **100%** sure that is all the *Buyer* is interested in then it is OK to have a one-item *Menu*. It happens but I find this to be extremely rare.

If we offer only one major benefit we cut out a significant part of the population that may be looking for another solution but are unaware you have it right there in front of you, **inadvertently creating a lower closing ratio.**

For example, if we say we can save the *Buyer* money and only 33% of the people are interested in that benefit we are leaving 67% of potential *Buyers* out of our solution. If we add to our *Menu* the point that we can also save them time and 33% are interested in that specific solution we have just doubled the population whom may be interested in our product, service or idea. Now if we additionally include in our *Menu* the point that they can also prevent headaches or problems and 33% are motivated by this benefit we now have 99% of the population who may be interested in our solution.

My friends this is how you can dramatically increase interest in your product, service or idea and therefore improve your closing ratio immediately!

An important fact is there is always more than one major benefit to buying/agreeing with any solution. You need to open your mind and explore the other benefits. Can you take the time before the *Buy-Sell-Encounter* to find the other solutions? It is critical folks.

2. Do the words "me", "I" or "we" appear in your answer above?

If so you need to remove them immediately. *The Menu* is a list of outward-based statements about the *Buyer*. Outward-based means <u>you are not in the picture</u>. Words such as "me", "I", "we" and "our" should never appear in *The Menu*. It is all about the *Buyer*!

Let me illustrate some examples of simple *Menus* before covering the rules. Pretend I am selling payroll services to a small business owner. Pay particular attention to the words I use. Notice also I will start with a *SOGI* so you get a feel for the flow.

SOGI – "It's crucial to **avoid** major mistakes that may land you in trouble with the IRS. (Gap Statement) We've been able to help a lot of clients avoid these mistakes and get other major benefits.

Menu-There are three major benefits to you for moving ahead with this project:

> First, you will experience a significant money savings

> Second, you may save at least two hours a day in lost time

> And finally you can prevent the headaches most business owners experience when changing payroll companies".

You'll notice it is all about the *Buyer*. In a way *The Menu* acts like a crystal ball showing what the future holds for them by buying/agreeing with us.

The word "you" is predominant. **An important concept is to make the *Buyer* the subject of every *Menu* statement!!**

52

Here is another real-life example. Let's say I am a father trying to convince my sixteen-year old daughter to improve her grades and avoid summer school. *The Menu* might go something like this:

SOGI – "It's important to you, not to have a miserable summer, am I right? I mention having a miserable summer because that is exactly where you are headed. You may have to go to summer school if your grades don't improve.

Menu-Honey, there are some possible negative outcomes to you if you have to go to summer school.

> "One, you will likely lose your cell phone"

> "Two, you'll be alone without your friends"

> "And three you may also lose your car if your grades don't significantly improve."

Now, you tell me, do I have my daughters attention? Is her interest in whatever I am talking about moving higher? Yes! Am I speaking to things that are very important to her? Absolutely. Are these *Menu* choices important to me? Not at all, but my solution is and I need to elevate **her** interest in my solution.

Let me re-emphasize; this is done by speaking to what is important to her, not me! Do I want to win the *Buy-Sell-Encounter* or do I want to talk about what is important to me? I want to win the *Buy-Sell-Encounter*. My chances of winning increase dramatically when I speak about her! The solution is also a *win/win* for both of us.

This is a good reminder that influence is 24/7, not just when you are selling for monetary gain. We need to be influential in all major areas of our life to ensure we are practicing good leadership in our community and providing real value and help to our family and friends.

Now is a good time to review the rules of *The Menu*.

- ✓ Make sure the statements are outward-based and all about what is in it for the *Buyer*. Ensure the words "me", "I", "our" or "we" are not in the *Menu*.

- ✓ If doing your *Menu* verbally, no more than three choices

- ✓ If doing your *Menu* formally (brochure, website or formal presentation) no more than five choices (there are a finite amount of benefits. HINT: Think about the four objections and work backwards to head them off prior with a good *Menu*!)

- ✓ Very Important: **Do not put anything in your *Menu* you cannot 100% deliver and prove you can deliver!** (Yes, I was screaming. It is that important.)

- ✓ Do not build a *Menu* that sounds good but is impossible to make happen!

A carefully crafted *Menu* will get the *Buyer* to say yes to your product, service or idea before you start talking about your product, service or idea!

Know this, we are just getting started. The *Buyer* has no idea what is in store for them! Look at what we have done so far. We are only seconds into any *Buy-Sell-Encounter* and we have laid out a series of great things the *Buyer* will get for agreeing with us!

What is your *Menu*? What are the powerful benefits I get for buying/agreeing with you? Craft a simple *Menu* below:

1._____

2._____

3._____

4._____

5._____

You present your *Menu* with power and confidence. What you do next is crucial. Now you need to ask the *Buyer* to select one and only one item off your *Menu*. It may sound something like this:

> "In considering these choices, which one seems to jump out as the most important to you?"

Or something like this:

> "You can get all four of these benefits but if you could have only one of these benefits which one would you choose?"

The *Buyer* will consider the *Menu* and then do something magical in the world of influence. They will select an item off your *Menu*!

Guess what just happened in the first few seconds of the Buy-Sell-Encounter...

They just bought from you! Just like in a restaurant they selected an item which means they have a certain level of interest in your product. **Sixty-Seconds to Yes**!

Let us go back to the restaurant so we can illustrate another major benefit of the *Menu*. If in the restaurant you do not see anything you like in the *Menu*, what can you do? Get up and leave. **You expressed a lack of need, want or desire in the first few moments of the restaurant experience.** This is one of the four objections and one that a *Seller* must not push or overcome this objection as this is manipulation.

The same holds true for our *Buyer* in our *Buy-Sell-Encounter*. Wouldn't it be wonderful to find that out up-front, before wasting the *Buyer* and *Sellers'* time?

The *Menu* does that! When a *Seller* presents the *Menu* and the *Buyer* sees no benefit for them in the *Menu* the *Buy-Sell-Encounter* is over...in the very beginning! How many presentations have we all sat through where we did not get a chance to say we are not interested until the end? The *Menu* eliminates one of the four objections in the first sixty-seconds of the *Buy-Sell-Encounter*, saving time for all involved.

You now need to do two things:

First, continue to elevate their interest to a maximum level and second, do not screw it up when it is time to prove your case and make your presentation (*Validation*).

Let us add to the role-play scenario we stared in chapter five. We will now add the *Menu* to the *Buy-Sell-Encounter*. Here is how that would look:

Exploration Phase

Seller: Thank you for the information about what is going on here at Acme Roofing. Being a dynamic company you must always be looking out to prevent customer service nightmares. (*SOGI* and official start to the *Buy-Sell-Encounter*)

I mention preventing nightmares because we've been able to do that for many clients. We'd like to do the same for you. (Gap statement before *Menu*)

You can experience three major benefits with the XR600 system. They are:

Saving money

Preventing unhappy clients due to lost calls

Save time through easy to operate systems

You may get all three, but if you had to select the most important, which would you make number one (have *Buyer* select Menu item)?

Buyer: I would have to say preventing unhappy clients.

You've set the hook, now you have to reel them in. We all know what can happen after the hook is set and we start reeling them in. Anything. If you have a purpose and a plan you can greatly increase the odds of winning the *Buy-Sell-Encounter*! You do have a purpose and a plan. Buckle up because here is where it gets good!

Chapter 7

The *Journey*

Purpose of the Journey: It has been said knowing **what** people want to buy will earn you a living. Knowing **why** people buy will make you rich! People do not just buy the "**what**", they buy the "**why**"! The *Journey* will help you discover the *Buyer*'s "why"! Knowing this arms you with a powerhouse of information which makes it difficult for the *Buyer* to say "no".

Position in the *Decision Process*:

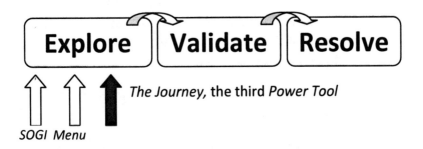

The Journey, the third *Power Tool*

SOGI Menu

The *Menu* we developed in the prior chapter is the "**what**". It tells the *Seller* what the *Buyer* may want from them. This is crucial but only part of the story. The *Journey* will uncover the "**why**", which finishes the story.

Many of my graduates consider the *Journey* the most important power tool. I agree. This is where the rubber meets the road in *The Decision Process*.

The *Menu* by itself is powerful but dangerous and here is why; the danger happens when the *Buyer* selects a *Menu* item. When the *Buyer* says "I need to save more money"

(*Menu* item) the *Seller* becomes eager to show how they can deliver on that promise.

The *Menu* item is only half the deal...the "**what**". The *Seller* needs to be patient and take the *Buyer*'s interest to an even **higher level**. The *Journey* will do just that. The *Journey* uncovers the "**why**", the most important piece of information uncovered in *The Decision Process*.

The *Journey* is the questioning methodology our training students learn. In an earlier chapter I discussed the fact that we do not ask qualifying questions in the *Buy-Sell-Encounter*. We have one specific goal in the *Buy-Sell-Encounter* and that is to get a yes to our solution we presented to the *Buyer*. Qualifying is *Exchange of Information and Direction* and therefore takes place outside the *Buy-Sell-Encounter.*

The questions we ask in the *Buy-Sell-Encounter* come with a **very specific purpose.**

To help Illustrate this purpose let us start with an analogy. I am sure you have read the book or seen one of the many iterations of the Charles Dickens classic, <u>A Christmas Carol.</u>

In the story as you will recall Ebenezer Scrooge is visited by three ghosts who take him on a "journey" to three places; Christmas past, Christmas present and Christmas future.

By exposing him to what happened (past), what the current situation is (present) and what will happen if he continues with his ways (future) the ghosts were able to persuade Mr. Scrooge to **change.**

The *Journey* methodology follows a similar path.

The name *"The Journey"* comes from the fact that you are going to take the *Buyer* on a *Journey* similar to Mr. Scrooge. The *Journey* is a trip that stops at two specific and distinct places:

"The Pit of Hell"

And

"Nirvana"

These two stops are metaphors (obviously) for the **only two answers** the *Seller* needs to discover and uncover from the *Buyer* in the *Journey*.

With these two pieces of critical information you will be able to navigate the *Buyer* through the rest of the *Decision Process* with power and confidence.

These two pieces of information are so important that you cannot continue the process without them as you will need them several more times in the *Buy-Sell-Encounter*.

Each step in the *Decision Process* moving forward is guided by these two pieces of information. You cannot complete *Validation* or *Resolution* properly without them, they are that important.

If you want to be eager and jump from the *Menu* to *Validation* and show how you can deliver the "what", you will diminish your chances of closing the deal because you did not get the *Buyer* to articulate out loud the "**why**". This is ok and does not always kill the deal.

It does not mean you will not win the encounter but if you do it is because the *Buyer* took them self on the *Journey* (it is a natural part of the *Decision Process*). It is natural and we all do it to some degree internally without the *Sellers'* help.

Every decision needs a powerful emotional bond for the *Buyer* to motivate them to take action and overcome the *Fear of Change*. That emotional bond, or as I call it the *Buyers Bond* is discovered and developed in the *Journey*.

How does this work in practical application? It is broken down into two sets of questions.

The first sequence of questions take the *Buyer* to the *Pit of Hell*, a metaphor for what will happen if the *Buyer* **does not** buy or agree with you.

The second sequence of question take the *Buyer* to *Nirvana*, a metaphor for what will happen if the *Buyer* does buy or agree with you.

Before I cover these two questioning sequences in more detail let me clarify an important point about the Journey. To illustrate I will use a story.

When I first moved to Southern California from Northern California, Rob, a friend of mine wanted to teach me how to surf. He was very good and I wanted to learn so I had a great attitude about surfing in sunny Southern California.

I considered myself a fairly coordinated person and of decent athletic ability (at the time!) so I thought how hard can it be? I can sense you know where this is going but allow me to finish for my own benefit and therapy...

Rob spent a fair amount of time with me on the beach patiently showing me how to go from a prone position on the board to a standing position. I practiced several times successfully and felt that I had a pretty good handle on the lesson taught.

Then we went into the surf, or as I now call it the freezing-pounding- shark-infested hell. What I quickly learned is no one can actually train you on how to surf. All the lessons in the world on the warm, stable beach cannot duplicate the reality of a constantly moving wave.

After what seemed like forever and a thousand wasted waves I finally managed to **almost** stand up for a millisecond before going head first into the cold, murky, shark-infested water...again. OK, maybe I had no real proof of sharks being in the area but I felt they were and that should be enough, right?

Here is the point, surfing is something you need to **feel and experience for yourself**. In the end no one can teach you what to expect or to instill the touch and feel needed to stand on the board. It takes time and effort. You will need a basic amount of knowledge that an instructor can give which shortens the time to value, but you still need to put in the time on the surf.

Tying this back into the *Journey,* the same methodology applies. I can tell you how it is supposed to work but in the end you will need to do it to experience it.

It is a skill to extract these two pieces of valuable information. Skill as we have mentioned takes time and proper practice.

You get a little better each time so do not get discouraged if you find yourself struggling with the *Journey* in the early stages of your development.

Let us dig into the method.

First stop; *Pit of Hell*. What I want you to imagine is you and the *Buyer* are standing at the top of stone stairs. You are looking down into the mouth of a dark, ominous cave. You are confident and unafraid as you take to *Buyer* by the arm and start leading them down into the cave towards the *Pit of Hell*. Overly Dramatic? Maybe, but stay with me.

This part of the *Journey* starts when you ask the *Buyer* to select a *Menu* item and then ask them why they selected that particular item. You are off on the Journey. You know this is where you are going so your confidence is high and you can then focus on the answers given.

The questions you ask will direct the *Buyer* down those stone stairs. In other words, you want to dig them into a negative hole.

The three phases you want to walk the *Buyer* through on the way to the *Pit of Hell* are:

What happened in the past as a result of not having the benefit selected the *Menu*?

What is the current state as a result of not having the benefit selected in the *Menu*?

What will continue to happen if they do not get the benefit selected in the *Menu*?

This is an important progression. Past, present and future. Just like Scrooge.

You may be tempted to take them just to the future and skip the past and present. I will warn you not to do this and for this reason; the past and present are **real**! These

64

are two things that **actually happened and are happening now**. The *Buyer* needs to articulate these out loud because if they say it out loud it will help them re-live the pain suffered in the past and the pain they are currently experiencing! This creates an enormous amount of emotion, which is what you want.

The future is not real **yet** so they will not have the same emotional connection but need to see where they will go if they do not get the selected *Menu* benefit.

The future is also very important because **that is the *Pit of Hell***. The future disaster is **the** single-most important piece of information you need to remember as you will use it several more times moving forward through the *Decision Process*.

Let me demonstrate a sequence of questions and how it may look in a sterile, Vacuum-like environment.

"I see you selected saving time as the most important benefit, why?"

"What happened to make you jump on that specific benefit?" (Past)

"What did that cause to happen?" (Past)

"Then what happened" (Past)

"What is happening today as a result?" (Present)

"What if that continues, what is going to happen?" (Future bad thing)

"What ultimately will that lead to?" (***Pit of Hell!!***)

Obviously this is just a simple illustrative example. This may take 30 seconds or three hours depending on the *Buyer* and magnitude of the decision.

The key for you to remember is this; are you sure you have taken them far enough down the dark cave to the *Pit of Hell*? The more powerful and emotional the answer the better your chance of getting a favorable decision.

Like surfing this looks easy to a skilled professional and awkward to a beginner. You need to practice and plan out your questions prior to the *Buy-Sell-Encounter*.

Many of my students ask the same question about this part of the questioning. They have concerns about us being too intrusive and personal. What gives us the right to take the *Buyer* to the *Pit of Hell*? This is a fair question and here is my response:

We earn the right to do this because we have a solution to prevent this from possibly happening again! That is why **we are here** in the *Buy-Sell-Encounter* to begin with. We are trying to show them our product, service or idea will **prevent bad things** (*Pit of Hell*).

Read the following paragraph slowly with full comprehension. Read it twice or more if need be until it fully resonates.

If the *Buyer* cannot articulate a bad thing that has happened and will continue to happen without the solution we are offering then our solution most likely will not be important enough for them to take action!

I know you only read that once. Go back and read it at least one more time. I get human nature since I am one myself, most of the time.

Moving on…

Once you are sure you've found the *Buyer's Pit of Hell* it is crucial you remember it. You will soon need it.

So, we took them to the *Pit of Hell* and remembered what this is for the *Buyer*. Now we can switch it up and take them to the happy place known as *Nirvana*.

It works the same but with a positive spin about what will happen if they buy/agree with your solution.

The *Journey* to *Nirvana* is all future-based. They cannot possibly be living with our benefit now or in the past because they just expressed what happened and what will happen by lacking the benefit you proposed. If they already had our benefit they would not have selected it off our *Menu*!

From the *Pit of Hell* we change direction towards *Nirvana*. We are now standing arm-in-arm with the *Buyer* at the foot of a white marble staircase, ascending up into a beautiful, bright place.

We start our questioning and begin stepping them up the stairs. They may sound something like this:

"Let's switch it around, what if you can save money, what does that mean for you?" (Future-based)

   "That is nice, but what does that change do for you?" (Future-based)

"What does that ultimately do for you, I mean, what is your goal 5-10 years from now" (***Nirvana***!!)

Again, this example is sterile and contrived simply to allow you to see how it may look. This may take 30 seconds or three years…only the *Buyer* and you know for sure.

Once you have the *Buyer's Nirvana* you will need to remember it!

Before we move to the final step in the *Exploration* phase let's look at a graphic of what the *Journey* looks like from above:

The *Journey* Graphic

Buyer selects *Menu* item (the "**What**")

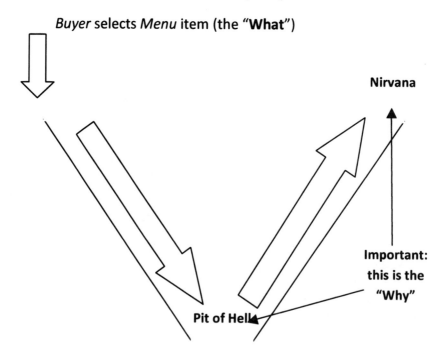

Nirvana

Important: this is the "Why"

Pit of Hell

Remember, we leave the Journey with three absolutely crucial pieces of information:

The *Menu* Item

The *Buyer's Pit of Hell* (What will happen if they do not get the benefit selected)

The *Buyer's Nirvana* (What will happen if they do get the benefit selected)

I will repeat the first phrase of this chapter: Knowing **what** people want to buy will earn you a living. Knowing **why** people buy will make you rich.

People use the "**what**" to get the "**why**".

When you go buy a drill at the hardware store **what** you bought is a drill. **Why** you bought is you really need a hole in a piece of wood to finish your daughter's new playhouse and have it be the envy of the neighborhood.

If you sell drills you can earn a living. If you sell the ability for a dad to fulfill his dream to build his daughter a beautiful playhouse you will be rich.

Summary: Before moving to the next chapter let's string together the *Power Tools* learned so far and see where we are in the *Decision Process*.

We start the *Buy-Sell-Encounter* with a *Statement of Great Importance*

> "It's crucial you don't end up in the 90% of businesses that fail in the first five years, am I right?"

We insert a gap statement to get to the **Menu**.

> "My clients have experienced success in avoiding this dreadful pitfall"

We launch into the *Menu*.

> "There are three major benefits to you by moving to Acme Payroll Services:
>
> First, **you** will save time on bothersome paperwork
>
> **You** will save money through more efficient systems
>
> **You** will avoid IRS payroll headaches
>
> Which of these hits home the most with you right now?"

Buyer selects *Menu* item. **By the way, they just bought from you!**

> "Why did you pick 'avoid IRS headaches' so fast? Something must be going on with you right now. What is it?"

Take *Buyer* to *Pit of Hell* and remember their answer.

Take *Buyer* to *Nirvana* and remember their answer.

Adding to our role-play scenario started in the previous two chapters we will now add the *Journey*. Here is what that may look like from the beginning:

:

Exploration

Seller: Thank you for the information about what is going on here at Acme Roofing. Being a dynamic company you must always be looking out to prevent customer service nightmares. (*SOGI* and official start to the *Buy-Sell-Encounter*)

I mention preventing nightmares because we've been able to do that for many clients. We'd like to do the same for you. (Gap statement before Menu)

You can experience three major benefits with the XR600 system. They are:

Saving money

Preventing unhappy clients due to lost calls

Save time through easy to operate systems

You may get all three, but if you had to select the most important, which would you make number one (have *Buyer* select Menu item)?

Buyer: I would have to say 'preventing unhappy clients'.

Seller: You seem to jump right on that one! What happened? (Intro into the *Journey* and directing the *Buyer* towards the *Pit of Hell*)

Buyer: Well, we just need to keep our clients happier.

Seller: Happier? What do you mean?

Buyer: In today's economic climate we need to hold on to all the customers we can.

Seller: What happens if you don't?

Buyer: Well, lost revenue. Lost revenue means laying crews off.

Seller: What impact will that have on the office?

Buyer: A huge blow to morale.

Selling: What happens then?

Buyer: I may be out of a job (*Pit of Hell*)!

Seller: Ouch, let's try to stop that! Switch it around, what if you had happier clients, what would that change (directing the *Buyer* to *Nirvana*)?

Buyer: Well, we might be able to hire more crews.

Seller: How does that change the game here?

Buyer: More crews means more money for everyone.

Seller: What does that do for you personally?

Buyer: More money means I can retire early and spend time with the grandkids (Nirvana).

You are now ready to finish *Exploration* with your fourth *Power Tool*, the *Commitment Statement*.

Chapter 8

The Commitment Statement

Purpose of the *Commitment Statement* – People will 100% buy when they have an **extreme** interest in a product, service or idea. People may buy with a mild to low interest, it is just more difficult for them to make a favorable decision. The *Commitment Statement* will drive the *Buyer*'s interest to the highest level. The *Buyer* will be on the edge of their seat, wondering how the *Seller* can make this happen!

Position in the *Decision Process*:

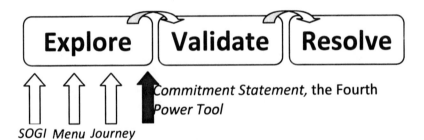

Up to now *Sellers* needed to see if there was any interest in their product and then were able to increase that interest by using three *Power Tools* of influence; the *SOGI, Menu* and *Journey*.

Let us wrap up the *Exploration* phase with a *Power Tool* that is simple but not simplistic.

The *Commitment Statement* is important because it takes the *Buyer* and the *Seller* from "I think I can help" to "**I know I can help**!"

This important transition sets the *Seller* up for success in *Validation*. It also creates the **highest** *Level of Interest the Buyer* will experience in the entire *Buy-Sell-Encounter*.

As mentioned in chapter three, once you are finished with *Exploration* the *Seller's* credibility and *Buyer's* interest will only go down. It is ok, it is natural. The plan is to mitigate that decrease, which is very manageable.

The *Commitment Statement* ties the entire *Exploration* phase into a neat little bow. It is easy to understand but difficult to accomplish if the *Seller* did not create a proper *Menu* and take the *Buyer* on the *Journey*.

The reason for this is simple; the *Commitment Statement* encompasses the selected *Menu* item, the *Pit of Hell* and *Nirvana*. If they are unknown, it is impossible to deliver correctly and powerfully.

The key to delivering the *Commitment Statement* is confidence. The *Seller* will have confidence because they have done their homework and know what they are about to say is 100% true.

There is much to say about the statement but first let me give you a sample of what a *Commitment Statement* looks like.

Let's say that the *Menu* item selected is saving time. In the *Journey* we discovered the *Pit of Hell* is the *Buyer* not seeing the family enough and missing the children growing up. *Nirvana* was being there for all the childrens' events.

After the *Journey* we can launch into *the Commitment Statement* and it might sound like this:

> "Thank **you** for sharing that valuable information. There is good news for **you**. Based on what **you** said **you** can save time with this idea, which **you** said will keep **you** from losing time with **your** family and get **you** closer to being there with **your** family for all the important events."

Pay close attention to the structure. The *Seller* is **not** in this statement. The word "you" in reference to the *Buyer* is all through the statement.

Breaking it down clearly what you say is this: "You can get (the *Menu* item), which will help prevent (*Pit of Hell*) and get you closer to (*Nirvana*).

My students usually chime in with concern at this point, indicating that we are over-extending ourselves.

Done correctly we are not, here is why; this is not a magic wand we wave and make this statement true. The *Buyer* has to do their part!

They need to keep their commitment and do their part, and their commitment starts with a key component; they need to buy first!

In short, the *Buyer* has a stake in making sure the *Pit of Hell* is avoided and *Nirvana* is achieved. Nothing will happen unless they first get the benefit posed in the *Menu*.

The *Seller* is comfortable with the *Commitment Statement* because they know they can 100% deliver the *Menu* item, **which is all they committed to**.

The genius (if I do say so myself) of the *Commitment Statement* is the key components (*Pit of Hell* and *Nirvana*) which are the most important part of the statement came from the **Buyer**! **This is what they said would happen if they didn't buy/agree and what would happen if they did buy/agree**! The *Seller* did not put words in the *Buyers'* mouth; they built your case for the *Seller*!

Here is semi-rhetorical question; how can they possibly say "no" at this point if the *Seller* has done the *Exploration* phase correctly? It is difficult to say "no", but what happens next will make it either more difficult to say "no" or very easy to say "no".

Here is a good time for a reminder as to what has just transpired through the *Exploration* phase; the *Seller* got the *Buyer* to an extreme *Level of Interest*, sitting on the edge of their seat and 100% ready to buy...though all that has transpired so far is having had the *Buyer* talk about themselves. This is a remarkable feat because you have not told the *Buyer* what the product, service or idea is!

Let us now include the *Commitment Statement* in our role-play scenario. Here is what that may look like from the beginning:

Exploration

Seller: Thank you for the information about what is going on here at Acme Roofing. Being a dynamic company you must always be looking out to prevent customer service nightmares. (*SOGI* and official start to the *Buy-Sell-Encounter*)

I mention preventing nightmares because we've been able to do that for many clients. We'd like to do the same for you. (Gap statement before Menu)

You can experience three major benefits with the XR600 system. They are:

Saving money

Preventing unhappy clients due to lost calls

Save time through easy to operate systems

You may get all three, but if you had to select the most important, which would you make number one (have *Buyer* select Menu item)?

Buyer: I would have to say 'preventing unhappy clients'.

Seller: You seem to jump right on that one! What happened? (Intro into the *Journey* and directing the *Buyer* towards the *Pit of Hell*)

Buyer: Well, we just need to keep our clients happier.

Seller: Happier? What do you mean?

Buyer: In today's economic climate we need to hold on to all the customers we can.

Seller: What happens if you don't?

Buyer: Well, lost revenue. Lost revenue means laying crews off.

Seller: What impact will that have on the office?

Buyer: A huge blow to morale.

Selling: What happens then?

Buyer: I may be out of a job (*Pit of Hell*)!

Seller: Ouch, let's try to stop that! Switch it around, what if you had happier clients, what would that change (directing the *Buyer* to *Nirvana*)?

Buyer: Well, we might be able to hire more crews.

Seller: How does that change the game here?

Buyer: More crews means more money for everyone.

Seller: What does that do for you personally?

Buyer: More money means I can retire early and spend time with the grandkids (Nirvana).

Seller: That is a wonderful plan. Thanks for sharing. I have good news; you can make your clients happier with less missed calls, which can keep you from not only losing your job but help you on your way to early retirement (Commitment Statement). Let's see how you can do that.

Finish strong! We are off to *Validation*. Time to prove your case!

Chapter 9

The *Impossible-To-Say-No-To Presentation*

Purpose of the *ITSNTP* – To maintain the *Buyer*'s interest and minimize the loss of credibility even while the *Seller* is talking about herself, product, service or idea. This methodology will help you organize your thoughts and present your case in the most powerful way to the *Buyer*.

Position in the *Decision Process*:

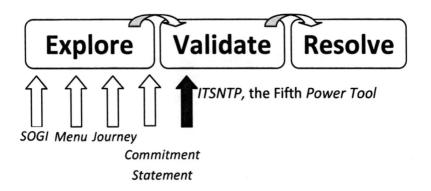

Let us begin by addressing the **"Spini Law of Credibility"**. It goes like this:

> **Your credibility decreases in direct proportion to the amount of talking you do!**

In other words the more *Sellers* talk, the more the *Buyer* loses interest.

The problem is we have to present our case and actually talk about our product, service or idea so how can we do so without killing the deal?

Simple, you will present your case but the fact is you will still be talking about the *Buyer* the entire time!

Another observation I have made over the years about *Sellers* presenting their case is they tend to focus on what **they** like about the product, service or idea. You already know this is wrong so no need to beat the dead horse on that one.

I want you to understand a powerful concept I call *The Credibility Curve*. This is the phenomenon whereby a *Seller's* credibility drops during the *Validation* phase of the *Decision Process*.

This is not a reason to panic as the amount it drops can be greatly mitigated by making a powerful and effective presentation. The better the presentation the more shallow the curve, the poorer the performance in *Validation* the steeper the curve.

Credibility Curve

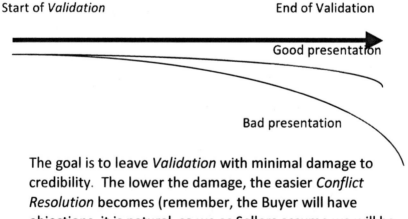

Start of *Validation*   End of Validation

Good presentation

Bad presentation

The goal is to leave *Validation* with minimal damage to credibility. The lower the damage, the easier *Conflict Resolution* becomes (remember, the Buyer will have objections, it is natural, so we as Sellers assume we will be moving from *Validation* to *Resolution*).

Remember the two forces at work in a decision:

Interest and **Defenses**

When one goes up the other goes down. They always work in complete opposite of each other. It is vital to keep defenses down and interest up.

What is the primary cause of the loss of credibility? It starts with the classic joke:

> Q. How do you know when a salesman is lying?

> A. His lips are moving.

Credibility drops when the *Buyers* **think** *Sellers* are not being truthful. Here is an important reminder to ponder; **Sellers get accused of lying even when they are telling the truth**.

What is the primary cause of this dynamic? When *Sellers* make **claims** vs. **facts**.

A common misunderstanding is a claim is a lie. A claim often can be a lie but not necessarily a lie. A claim can also be 100% true. What makes it a claim is not whether it is true or not, but rather the *Buyer* does not necessarily believe it, therefore it lacks credibility.

This happens inadvertently because *Sellers* expect that when they say something, the *Buyer* should believe it. In that case no need to submit ***Proof & Evidence***, right? Wrong.

It is important to ensure we are not dealing in claims in the *Decision Process*, ever. Deal only in facts.

Let's compare a fact to a claim:

Fact	_Claim_
True	May Be True
Provable	Difficult to Prove
Credible	Not Credible
Indisputable	Questionable

Are you presenting facts or claims? It is no more difficult to deal in facts than it is to deal in claims but I think you see the important differences between the two.

IMPORTANT: A claim becomes a fact to the _Buyer_ when they believe it to be true, not you.

A claim becomes a fact when the Seller presents _Proof & Evidence_ to support the fact.

The _Fact Formula_ looks like this:

Claim + Proof/Evidence = Fact

Not a difficult concept to follow but when we get lazy we tend to leave out the _Proof & Evidence._ I do not ever want my _Buyer_ to question the **validity** of my facts.

Let us do an exercise. I am going to make statements below and I want you to decide if they are facts or claims:

Statement	Circle One
This book has 14 chapters	fact or claim
This book is about selling and influence	fact or claim
This chapter addresses the *Validation* phase	fact or claim
This is the best book on selling ever written	fact or claim

If you said they are all facts you would be right. (Ok, maybe the last one has a hint of a claim!)

You get the picture. The first three statements are easily provable even if you are not 100% convinced they are true. The last statement (although I think it is true) is much more difficult to prove.

Facts do not need to be exciting or colorful. They are by nature sterile and logical. They need to appeal to the brain, remember? **The benefits to the *Buyer* that come with the facts need to be exciting and colorful and directed back to the heart!**

Let us move forward and see how it is supposed to look. Remember in the previous four chapters, we built a system to greatly elevate the *Buyer*'s interest. I showed you a four-step process to do so.

During that process we garnered three very important pieces of information; the *Menu* item, the *Pit of Hell* and *Nirvana*.

I told you how important it is to remember those three items as we will be using them throughout the remainder of the *Decision Process*. This is one of those times.

The question is who builds our presentation for us? The answer is simple; the *Buyer*. **We are only going to present the facts about our product, service or idea that are important to the *Buyer* based on the three answers they gave in the *Exploration* phase.**

The reason it is call the *Impossible-To-Say-No-To-Presentation* is the *Buyer* built it for us, *Sellers* merely present it back to them in an organized manner and pay particular attention to highlight the benefits.

Speaking of benefits, *Sellers* sometime forget to include the benefit with the fact. What makes this a bad thing is we do not buy facts, we buy benefits. Failing to highlight the benefit leaves the *Buyer* in a position to decide what the benefits may be and that is a bad thing. Let me illustrate.

If I am selling a commercial printer and I say as a provable fact that it produces 200 black and white copies a minute, what is a good thing you can say about that? Now, what is a possible negative about that? Did you find it easy to come up with both?

Taking that example, if the *Seller* tags a benefit to the fact for the *Buyer* it would look like this:

"This specific printer can produce 200 black and white copies a minute, which will save you a lot of time and that time can be spent on revenue-generating activities for your business rather than printing functions. "

Sellers want to ensure to tag each fact with a benefit for the *Buyer* so their mind does not drift into what may be a negative thought about the fact. If *Sellers* put the good into the *Buyer*'s mind they are more likely to only see the good in the product, service or idea.

The concept of benefit tagging is powerful, but only 50% of the equation. The other half is knowing which facts and benefits to use.

We already know which facts to use because the *Buyer* gave us the answer. The following statement is another one of those "really important" paragraphs that need your full attention and comprehension.

The facts we use are the ones that address the *Menu* item selected. *Sellers* should only present the facts relevant to the *Menu* item because that is what the *Buyer* said was most important to them.

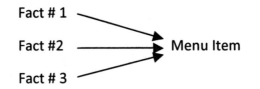

Another important concept is regarding the benefits. **The benefits associated with the facts address preventing the *Pit of Hell* and delivering *Nirvana*.**

Always tag a benefit statement to a fact (*Benefit Tagging*).

Here are some examples of how this works:

The product: A commercial printer.

The *Menu*:

- Save time with high-speed printing

- Save money through a less-expensive process

- Security in knowing there is a 100% guarantee or we'll buy the printer back.

In the following example let us say the *Menu* item was security from being stuck with something they do not like, their *Pit of Hell* we uncovered was too much wasted time and their *Nirvana* is selling the business and retiring early.

A fact/benefit statement would sound like this:

> "We include a 100% money back guarantee (fact) which allows you the security of knowing you won't be stuck with something you don't need (*Menu* item) and you won't be wasting time (*Pit of Hell*) trying to resolve problems. This time savings will allow you to focus on more revenue, driving up the value of your business and get you on your way to early retirement (*Nirvana*).

You will notice a fact/benefit statement is similar to the *Commitment Statement*. Exactly, *Sellers* will constantly remind *Buyers* they can satisfy their needs and deliver their wants. That's the whole point!

When it comes to how many fact/benefit statements to use I will help you understand this with a little story.

Many people don't know this about me but I was an LAPD reserve officer for a decade. I went through the entire academy and held many patrol assignments. I also had the privilege of being a self-defense instructor for new recruits.

In this class we first taught the LAPD Use of Force policy. At the time there were five steps in the Use of Force policy. They are in order of least severe to most severe:

Verbalization ("Stop and put your hands up!")

Firm Grip

Compliance (Wrist locks, pepper spray etc)

Combative/Aggressive (Baton, kicks, punches)

Deadly Force (You get the point)

The question is who decides what level of force is used? **The suspect, not the officer.**

The official policy statement at the time was "Officer shall use enough force that is reasonable and necessary to overcome resistance and affect the arrest." Anything more than this was considered excessive force and most likely a crime.

The point is this; how many facts should *Sellers* use? Only enough to overcome the *Buyer*'s resistance and affect the decision in a favorable way. That is a fancy was of saying keep it brief, do not over sell and talk yourself out of the deal!

I try not to exceed three facts/benefits for a single *Menu* item before I test the waters with closing statements. I use three maximum as four is overkill and *Buyers* seldom remember more than three anyway.

It is not the number used but the power in the fact/benefit statement that is important.

The proof *Sellers* submit will nail down the facts. *Sellers* need to have plenty of supporting proof such as credible statistics, facts and testimonials along with the ability to demonstrate if needed.

Only present proof that it necessary to certify the fact in the *Buyer's* mind.

Here is where important homework comes into play. Know the facts associated with proving all of the promises made in your *Menu*. This is called the *Menu Matrix*.

Sellers need the ability to build a custom presentation for the *Buyer* in seconds, after the *Exploration* phase is done! This is a skill that requires significant and proper practice and is totally possible but only if *Sellers* know their facts as they relate to the *Menu*.

Let us add to the role-play scenario and include two *Fact/Benefit Statements*, starting from the beginning:

Exploration

Seller: Thank you for the information about what is going on here at Acme Roofing. Being a dynamic company you must always be looking out to prevent customer service nightmares. (*SOGI* and official start to the *Buy-Sell-Encounter*)

I mention preventing nightmares because we've been able to do that for many clients. We'd like to do the same for you. (Gap statement before Menu)

You can experience three major benefits with the XR600 system. They are:

Having money

Preventing unhappy clients due to lost calls

Save time through easy to operate systems

You may get all three, but if you had to select the most important, which would you make number one (have *Buyer* select Menu item)?

Buyer: I would have to say 'preventing unhappy clients'.

Seller: You seem to jump right on that one! What happened? (Intro into the *Journey* and directing the *Buyer* towards the *Pit of Hell*)

Buyer: Well, we just need to keep our clients happier.

Seller: Happier? What do you mean?

Buyer: In today's economic climate we need to hold on to all the customers we can.

Seller: What happens if you don't?

Buyer: Well, lost revenue. Lost revenue means laying crews off.

Seller: What impact will that have on the office?

Buyer: A huge blow to morale.

Selling: What happens then?

Buyer: I may be out of a job (*Pit of Hell*)!

Seller: Ouch, let's try to stop that! Switch it around, what if you had happier clients, what would that change (directing the *Buyer* to *Nirvana*)?

Buyer: Well, we might be able to hire more crews.

Seller: How does that change the game here?

Buyer: More crews means more money for everyone.

Seller: What does that do for you personally?

Buyer: More money means I can retire early and spend time with the grandkids (Nirvana).

Seller: That is a wonderful plan. Thanks for sharing. I have good news; you can make your clients happier with less missed calls, which can keep you from not only losing your job but help you on your way to early retirement (Commitment Statement). Let's see how you can do that.

Validation

Seller: The XR600 has a 99.7% uptime rating from Consumer magazine (*Fact*), making it the highest ranking system of its kind. This means you won't have as many dropped calls and unhappy customers which you said will help protect your job (*Benefit*)!

Next the XR600 allows your staff to see who is calling by name (*Fact*). When they answer the phone and know the name the client has a better disposition about your company. A better disposition means more business, more money and early retirement (*Benefit*)!

In summary every *Buy-Sell-Encounter* requires some preparation. The bigger the event the more preparation needed. Do not wing it as you will come across as not credible and decrease your chances to win a decision in your favor.

Take massive action and get busy!

Chapter 10

Defense Diffusion

Purpose of *Defense Diffusion* – It's important before *Sellers* leave *Validation* to ensure they keep the *Buyer*'s interest as high as possible and defenses as low as possible. If defenses are high leaving *Validation* it makes it more difficult to resolve objections in *Conflict Resolution*. *Defense Diffusion* gives *Sellers* a tool to lower the *Buyer*'s defenses and better position them to make a decision in your and their favor.

Position in the *Decision Process*:

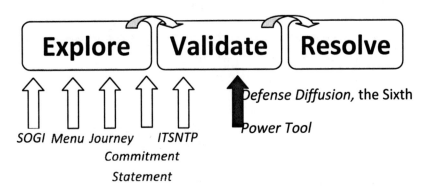

We will explore a concept that most people are very familiar with:

Risk vs. Reward

The basic principle is simple; the higher the risk the higher the reward. In this world we need to accept the fact that if we want to make great gains we need to put a lot on the line. The theory is risk and reward move up and down together; when risk goes up reward goes up, when risk is low the reward is low.

High risk / high reward is not for everyone as we know. In the area of building wealth only 1% of the population in the U.S. are defined as wealthy at age 65. These are the real risk takers. 99% never get there.

Most likely in our *Buy-Sell-Encounters* we will be dealing with many in the 99%, so we do not want to chase them off in the *Decision Process* by exposing them to **perceived** excessive risk if we do not need to. People generally hate change, remember? To change is to risk.

In order to bring defenses down while in the *Decision Process* we need to create a different dynamic. We need to show risk and reward from an **inverse perspective and relationship**. Stay with me here...

What we will develop is a tool that shows the *Buyer* **higher reward for less risk**. We will move these two forces **opposite** of each other, in defiance to conventional thinking.

The *Seller* will position this methodology just before asking closing questions and head into *Conflict Resolution*.

The *Defense Diffusion* in a way becomes the last thing the *Buyer* remembers about *Validation*. It will nail down the entire *Validation* phase and leave the *Buyer* remembering this one thing about the product, service or idea.

Here is the basic concept; if the *Buyer* knew there was a **100% chance** the product, service or idea could deliver the benefit presented in the *Menu* and the *Validation* phase the *Buyer* would be 100% compelled to buy / agree.

The compelling desire drops proportionately as the guarantee percentage drops.

Let me walk you through this; if the *Buyer* thinks there is a 10% (low) chance the product, service or idea will work for them (reward) there is a 90% (high) chance they will not buy (risk). The *Buyer* would see this as 90% risk for 10% reward. Not a good deal.

If there is a 50% chance in the *Buyer*'s mind it will work then there is a 50% chance they will take favorable action and so on and so on...you get the picture.

The question remains; what can you do to move the reward component as close to 100% as possible and the risk component as close to 0% as possible?

The answer is a *Performance Guarantee*. Can *Sellers* offer a high level of certainty that the product, idea or service will do what they say? The answer is yes, but the variable is to what degree.

There are two types of *Performance Guarantees*.

1. **Promise to return the *Buyer* to their original state**

2. **100% satisfaction guarantee.**

If the *Seller* promises to return the *Buyer* to their original state if they are unhappy with the product, service or idea they take away the risk of **bad change**, guaranteeing them the only change they will experience is **good change** or no change at all. This is a powerful method to diffuse defenses.

As the *Seller* wraps up *Validation* and wants to interject this type of *Performance Guarantee* it might sound like this:

"John, if you are not 100% pleased with the results we'll buy our printer back, remove it at our expense and return your old printer in its original state."

Another example might look like this (speaking to my daughter about increasing her grades to avoid summer school):

"Honey, if you follow the path I outlined for better grades and put forth an honest effort and your grades still don't improve you may keep your cell phone and car for the summer (her original state)."

After you deliver this promise you then ask them closing questions to test the water. More on that later.

The second methodology, the 100% guarantee method states that if the *Buyer* is not completely happy with the product, service or idea they will get an additional reward or payout above and beyond the original product, service or idea.

This might sound something like this:

"If after you complete my training program and it doesn't exceed your expectations you can have a full refund and take the program over again at our expense."

This is the actual guarantee we offer in my individual and corporate training contract. To date no one has ever exercised the offer (fact) but it stands.

Another example:

"If not completely satisfied we will come in and do additional training for your staff at our expense, focusing specifically on the areas we believe need targeted help."

We are simply adding additional benefits if we are not making the *Buyer* happy or satisfied.

I will stress again this is how *Sellers* want to finish *Validation*. That way the *Buyer* will be headed to *Conflict Resolution* with this *Performance Guarantee* swimming around in their head as the last thing they heard. If done correctly their defenses are greatly muted and interest will remain high.

OK, the *Seller* has navigated the *Buyer* through the first two phases of the *Decision Process; Exploration and Validation*.

Now it is time to ask for the decision. Here is the exact point to ask for the decision; just after *Validation*.

It is a universally known fact that we have heard our entire adult lives; most business is lost because the salesperson fails to ask for the business.

That won't be us now will it!

Closing is no mystery. There are books written on closing because people are looking for some magical pill or formula to get the *Buyer* to say yes.

If you remember the foundation of this program you will know the decision to buy has already been made. You just need to make it stick.

To close the *Buyer* and ask for the decision there is a simple and easy way to do it.

The *Seller* will ask a couple of quick, easy-to-answer questions to gauge the temperature of the *Buyer*.

Examples are "How does it sound so far?" -or- "How do you want your name to appear on the contract?"

Do not get bogged down in some weird, technical formula for closing. None of them are worth a penny.   Walk them through a couple of simple questions. That is all you need to do!

Here is what makes your attitude different and your confidence so high compared to your competition; **you expect them to say no and have objections**, even though you did a masterful job in *Exploration* and *Validation*!

You know the party is just beginning and we need to resolve conflict before the real decision can be made in your favor. Go back to the aircraft carrier example. You expect the flight is not over and are ready to take off again if needed.

If by chance the *Buyer* says "Let's do it!" you may be pleasantly surprised but surprised nonetheless!

We will now add *Defense Diffusion* to the role-play scenario, starting from the beginning:

Exploration

Seller: Thank you for the information about what is going on here at Acme Roofing. Being a dynamic company you must always be looking out to prevent customer service

---

nightmares. (*SOGI* and official start to the *Buy-Sell-Encounter*)

I mention preventing nightmares because we've been able to do that for many clients. We'd like to do the same for you. (Gap statement before Menu)

You can experience three major benefits with the XR600 system. They are:

Saving money

Preventing unhappy clients due to lost calls

Save time through easy to operate systems

You may get all three, but if you had to select the most important, which would you make number one (have *Buyer* select Menu item)?

Buyer: I would have to say 'preventing unhappy clients'.

Seller: You seem to jump right on that one! What happened? (Intro into the *Journey* and directing the *Buyer* towards the *Pit of Hell*)

Buyer: Well, we just need to keep our clients happier.

Seller: Happier? What do you mean?

Buyer: In today's economic climate we need to hold on to all the customers we can.

Seller: What happens if you don't?

Buyer: Well, lost revenue. Lost revenue means laying crews off.

Seller: What impact will that have on the office?

Buyer: A huge blow to morale.

Selling: What happens then?

Buyer: I may be out of a job (*Pit of Hell*)!

Seller: Ouch, let's try to stop that! Switch it around, what if you had happier clients, what would that change (directing the *Buyer* to *Nirvana*)?

Buyer: Well, we might be able to hire more crews.

Seller: How does that change the game here?

Buyer: More crews means more money for everyone.

Seller: What does that do for you personally?

Buyer: More money means I can retire early and spend time with the grandkids (Nirvana).

Seller: That is a wonderful plan. Thanks for sharing. I have good news; you can make your clients happier with less missed calls, which can keep you from not only losing your job but help you on your way to early retirement (Commitment Statement). Let's see how you can do that.

Validation

Seller: The XR600 has a 99.7% uptime rating from Consumer magazine (*Fact*), making it the highest ranking system of its kind. This means you won't have as many dropped calls and unhappy customers which you said will help protect your job (*Benefit*)!

Next the XR600 allows your staff to see who is calling by name (*Fact*). When they answer the phone and know the name the client has a better disposition about your company. A better disposition means more business, more money and early retirement (*Benefit*)!

Let me show you our "No loss guarantee". If our system doesn't exceed your expectations in the first 30 days we'll re-install your old system at our expense and give you a full refund. (*Defense Diffusion*)

How does it all sound so far (Closing question)?

Let us move the *Buyer* through *Conflict Resolution* with grace, power, ease and confidence.

Chapter 11

ARCH

Purpose of *ARCH* – In the first phase of the *Decision Process, Exploration,* the *Buyer* becomes emotionally connected to the *Seller* and the product, service or idea and interest is raised to a high level. In the previous two chapters the *Seller* presented the case as to why the decision to move forward is valid. The *Seller* ended the second, or *Validation* phase of the *Decision Process* by asking for the decision but fully expecting to move into the third and final phase of *the Decision Process, Conflict Resolution.*

Conflict Resolution connects the *Buyer* to the *Seller* in another way which is the most powerful dynamic in the *Decision Process.* The *Buyer* develops **trust** with the *Seller.* Trust is critical if the *Seller* is to be successful in navigating the *Buyer* through to the end.

The next chapter will give the *Seller* powerful methods to overcome objections and successfully navigate conflict. However, knowing how to resolve conflict and overcome objections effectively is only half the situation. *Buyers* will constantly throw up smokescreens and mislead the *Seller.* This is not out of malice or bad will, but rather fostered by the number one objection, *Fear of Change.*

Too many *Sellers* do what I call "chase the ghost". They try and handle all objections without first finding out if the objection is **real**. ARCH will help the *Seller* find the real objection in a powerful flow that unveils what is really troubling the *Buyer.*

Position in the *Decision Process*:

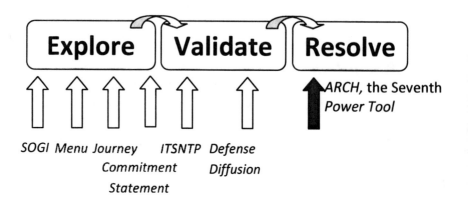

Before developing the *ARCH* methodology I want to spend the next several pages back-filling more information and guidelines for successful navigation through *Conflict Resolution* and overcoming objections. Remember, we do not handle objections or make them go away, we overcome them. They are always present and never diminish in weight, the *Seller* simply established the *Value* higher than the *Cost*.

Value ≥ Cost = favorable decision (win/win)

This formula was developed in chapter 3 so now is a good time to bring it back into play.

First, a **Warning**: *ARCH* is a very powerful tool. If a *Seller* truly masters this methodology, it will be difficult for them to ever lose an argument. This is not necessarily a good thing! In addition to being annoying it can be perceived as manipulation.

In my training facilities I have posted on the walls two rules for all participants to see. There are:

1. When starting *Conflict Resolution* never try to overcome objections first

2. If you really want to overcome objections first, refer to Rule # 1

Resolving conflict and overcoming objections involves certain attitudes. This first of which is **patience**. When the *Seller* is over eager to pounce on an objection the *Buyer* sees this as having canned responses, therefore not really concerned about her hesitation or fears.

In addition, if the *Seller* tries to solve the problem and it is not the **real** problem the *Buyer* knows they have an advantage and will play the *Seller* like a fine Stradivarius violin. Knowing the *Seller* is "chasing a ghost" gives the Buyer the upper hand in knowing the problem or objection is unsolvable because it is not real! **You will never get there dealing with a fake objection.**

Understand the *Buyer* is most likely dealing with *Fear of Change*, which makes people operate under a certain level desperation. If the *Seller* shows patience and lets the situation unfold, a powerful dynamic of **trust** evolves.

As the tide turns and the *Buyer* begins to articulate what is really bothering him the **Seller** moves from trying to sell something to a **consultant**.

Know this, finding the real objection or concern does not mean we can solve the problem or overcome it. There are hopeless situations. There are times when the *Fear of Change* is so great we cannot move the *Buyer* beyond it.

This is ok, it is never going to be 100% successful nor does it need to be for us to be powerful and influential. There is however great value in knowing what the real problem or objection is as quickly as possible.

Allow me to illustrate a very important concept that is crucial to success in *Conflict Resolution* and throughout the *Decision Process*. Let me share a bit of ancient history first.

In around 350 B.C. a King (King Philip II to be specific) was out and about conquering the known world. This apparently was a popular pastime for world rulers in those days.

Well, the known world at the time centered around the Mediterranean Sea.

King Philip II's army landed on the northern shore of the Isle of Greece. They started doing their conquering starting from north to south.

As they proceeded south they ventured into a little territory known as **Laconia**.

The capital of this region was a city called **Sparta**. If you know anything about ancient world history or Sparta you probably know where this is heading, but humor me for those not fully up-to-speed.

The region of Laconia and the city of Sparta were protected by their own army know as the Spartans. The Spartans were without question the fiercest warriors on the planet.

Many war historians believe that they are considered the best military machine in the history of the world and that they still would stack up today as the absolute best warriors.

In short, they kicked serious butt.

The story goes that King Philip II sent a messenger to the king of Sparta demanding Sparta surrender. The messenger stood before the king and started reading the demands set forth by King Philip II. The message started with the phrase, "If you don't lay down your weapons…".

The messenger then proceeded to list the many bad things that would happen to Laconia if the Spartans did not surrender. This went on for a while and the Spartan king listened patiently for the messenger to finish.

Once finished, the Spartan king carefully crafted his response back to King Philip II and gave it to the messenger for return delivery.

The messenger took the scroll back to King Philip II. King Philip unrolled the scroll and read the message from the Spartan king.

The message back to King Philip II had only one word:

"If"

That was it.

This incident is well known in the historical wonk circle as history's biggest "thumbing of the nose" (I have another analogy using a different digit of the hand but I need to keep it clean here. You're probably tracking way ahead of me anyway).

You see, the Spartans were long and fierce in the ways of war but extremely brief in speech.

From this incident a new word was born. The word is "laconic", named for the region protected by Sparta. Laconic means **brief in speech and words**.

The point is, like the Spartans we need to be brief in speech and words and long on action and resolve in *Conflict Resolution*. This is good rule throughout the *Decision Process* but critical here.

Here are the reasons for this:

First, words are like links in a chain; the more links we use the weaker the chain. When we are handling objections and we use too many words or talk too much, we start to sound defensive or we sound like we are justifying our product, service or idea. We do not need to do this. We believe in the product, service or idea and the value has already been established early on in the *Decision Process*.

Second, beyond brief speech and words is an even more powerful tool for handling conflict and overcoming objections, yet unfortunately the least used. Are you guessing what that tool might be?

Silence. In our eagerness to handle objections we often do not give the *Buyer* enough time or credit to work things out on their own. What I found is sometimes people will say an objection but not mean it; they were just thinking out loud.

In chapter 12, I will show you two places where silence is mandatory and very powerful when used properly.

Silence is not a popular concept among sales professionals because we like to talk by nature. If influential people have the discipline to use this tool effectively, you need to have that discipline too.

Another point that needs to be understood is the rule of persistence. There is a key concept for you to embrace and that is this:

Never, ever, ever agree with an objection. Read this ten times out loud!

It is OK to change from *Seller* to *Buyer* and leave the *Buy-Sell-Encounter* buying the "**no**" but never **buy the objection**. Here is why; the *Seller* had a product, service or idea that the *Buyer* said was good for them and they still said "no".

How can we agree with the objection? If the *Seller* agrees as to why the *Buyer* said no then the *Seller* did not really believe in her product, service or idea. It is fine the *Seller* didn't end with a *win/win*, but the *Seller* must never validate the excuse for not moving forward.

You and the *Buyer* are in *Conflict Resolution* together, but in two very distinct and different roles. I will use a semi-gross analogy to describe the relationship; imagine you are on a cruise ship and you see someone leaning over the rail with a strong bout of motion sickness (get it?). The role you want to play is to walk up, put your arm around their shoulder and say "I know how you feel and I want to help". This is called **empathy**. Conversely what too many *Sellers* do is walk up to the sick person and join them in vomiting over the rail. This is called **sympathy**. We want to be empathetic and help not sympathetic and join them in agreeing with the objection.

Believe in what you are doing, selling and creating for the *Buyer*. It is good for them or you would not be offering it up.

Another important attitude when engaging in *Conflict Resolution* is confidence. You must show power and leadership, even if you are not 100% comfortable yet with overcoming objections.

When I graduated from the Los Angeles Police Academy and was assigned my first watch I remember being so excited to be in a Black & White patrolling the streets of Los Angeles. Several hours into the shift we get what is called a "code 3" call. This is a true emergency and allows the police to get to the scene with lights and sirens and without regard for laws (i.e. we can run through red lights as safely as possible).

It was a shooting in progress and a victim was down. My adrenaline was pumping and I was excited to get to the scene! My partner was driving since she knew the area better than me. The shooting took place at a housing project in South Central Los Angeles called Nickerson Gardens. I remember coming around the corner and witnessing a scene of pure chaos; people screaming at each other, people crying and running down the street.

As I watched I started to buy into the chaos. As we stopped and got out of the vehicle my heart rate rose and for a minute I had a strange thought; someone better call the police so they can get here and handle this! That is when it hit me like a ton of lead...I **was** the police! I am the guy they called to handle the situation! I managed to pull it together (thanks to a good partner) and we brought the crowd under control and resolved the situation.

Imagine though if I did not re-group and instead joined in the chaos. How disturbing that would have been for the citizens who trust the police to handle these incidents on their behalf if I showed up and acted like they did. When we took charge the energy of the crowd decreased dramatically and a calming effect took over. Our confidence created a sedative-like effect on the crowd, thus enabling us to better manage the conflict.

Sellers need to do the same thing when engaged in *Conflict Resolution* with the *Buyer*. The *Seller* needs to keep the energy level low and calm. Here are two additional guidelines to follow:

- ✓ Never engage the *Buyer* in an argument during *Conflict Resolution*; it is counter-productive and raises the energy level

- ✓ Avoid using the words "but" and "however" as they by design are argumentative

Now that your attitude is one of patience and confidence let us explore my favorite *Power Tool* and the first step in navigating the *Buyer* through *Conflict Resolution;* The *ARCH* methodology!

ARCH is an acronym. Here it is in its entirety:

A > **A**cknowledge

R > **Re**-state

C > **C**larify

H > **H**ypothetical Solution

The *Seller* is going to guide the *Buyer* through a four-step process that will on the surface appear conversational but will have a powerful psychological impact on uncovering the truth about what may be bothering the *Buyer*.

Step One – *Acknowledge*

When the *Buyer* gives the *Seller* an objection or disagrees, the first step the *Seller* needs to do is *Acknowledge* the *Buyer* and let them know they heard them. I said they heard them, **not agree with them**. This is a simple and very quick step. Here are some basic examples of Acknowledgement:

" I hear you…"

"I appreciate that…"

"I understand…"

"Mmm Hmm.."

None of these statements indicate the *Seller* agrees with the *Buyer*. They are simply soft landings to position the *Seller* for the next step.

Step Two – *Re-state* the objection

This is a subtle yet critical step in the *ARCH* methodology. Once the *Seller* creates a soft landing with *Acknowledgement* they need to immediately respond with a *Re-statement*. For example, if the *Buyer* says they don't have the money right now an *Acknowledgement* and *Re-statement* would sound something like this:

Buyer – "I don't have the funds to allocate to this project."

Seller – "I hear you (*Acknowledge*), it's important to invest your money wisely (*Re-state*)."

This simple example requires an in-depth study because a lot has happened that we need to explore.

Remember a core rule is to never agree with an objection. If you read the example again you will find the *Seller* did not agree at all, but (important dynamic) the *Buyer* may think they did!

When the *Seller Re-states* it sounds like agreement, but the *Seller* is doing something subtle yet very important; the *Seller* is telling the *Buyer* their concern is heard (*Acknowledge*) and then *Re-states* the objection in a manageable way for the *Seller*! Read the last sentence again. The *Seller* needs to take an unsolvable objection and *Re-state* it in a way that is solvable. When the *Buyer* said they couldn't allocate funds the *Seller* turned that into making sure the *Buyer* invests wisely.

You see, we as *Sellers* cannot overcome "I don't have the money" but we can solve "investing wisely". We cannot overcome "I don't have the time" but can solve "investing time wisely". The *Seller* is creating the impression in the *Buyers'* mind that they are on the *Buyers* side (which is true, but not necessarily the way the *Buyer* thinks).

Some may think we are manipulating what the *Buyer* is saying by *Re-stating* their objection. We are not, we are merely *Re-stating* and positioning their concern in a manner which is solvable and addressing what the *Buyer* is most-likely really saying to us! I believe when someone is telling me they do not have the money that what they really mean is the investment value is not yet high enough to overcome the cost objection. When the *Buyer* tells me they do not have the time what they are really saying is the time investment value is not yet high enough to overcome the cost objection.

Keep in mind the purpose of *ARCH* is first to find out if the *Buyer* is telling us the truth or are they throwing up a smoke screen to mask the *Fear of Change*. It is designed to find the real objection or concern. We are not trying to resolve any objection yet. This is important to keep in mind. As a refresher from earlier in this chapter do not be eager to solve a problem that is not real!

After the *Seller Acknowledges* and *Re-states* the objection in a manageable way, we are ready for the next step.

Third Step – *Clarify* the objection

 Here is where the *Seller* asks the *Buyer* to clarify the objection. The *Seller* will ask a question or two about the objection to ensure the *Seller* fully understands the *Buyer's* concern. It also serves another purpose; it allows the *Seller* to buy some time and re-group. This prep time is crucial because if the objection turns out to be a real concern and not a smokescreen we need to have our response ready to go and delivered with confidence. We will work on that part of *Conflict Resolution* in the next chapter.

The *Clarify* integrated into our example step might sound something like this:

Buyer – "I don't have the funds to allocate to this project."

Seller – "I hear you (*Acknowledge*), it's important to invest your money wisely (*Re-state*)."

Seller – "What is it about the cost that bothers you?"

The *Seller* asks for clarification and then allows the *Buyer* time to respond. Let the *Buyer* speak as long as they want. You want the *Buyer* to start talking about themselves during the *ARCH* process. It might result in them resolving the objection on their own. This happens a lot. Remember it is a *Decision Process* the *Buyer* goes through, not a selling process!

Although we have them clarify, we are not doing this for the purpose of solving the objection at that point. This is a temptation for *Sellers*; we want to fix things as quickly as possible. This is where patience is important.

The first three steps of *ARCH* take only a few seconds. These few short seconds are powerful and important in navigating the *Buyer* successfully through *Conflict Resolution*. **They set the cornerstone of trust**. We then move to the fourth step in the *ARCH* methodology.

Fourth Step – *Hypothetical Solution*

Buckle up because here is where it gets good. What the *Seller* is about to do now will change the dynamic of the *Buy-Sell-Encounter* and put the *Buyer* on notice that the *Buy-Sell-Encounter* is not done quite yet.

Remember, the *Buyer* may be coming from *a Fear of Change* objection and they just want you to go away so they can hide behind that fear. On the other hand, the Buyer may have a real concern or objection and want to see how the *Seller* will deal with it. The *Hypothetical Solution* allows the *Seller* to find out which one it really is.

Here is the philosophy behind the *Hypothetical Solution*; humans will reveal their true feelings when backed into a corner. This sounds like an unfriendly practice perhaps but remember the *Seller* is trying to help the *Buyer*. Also, done correctly the *Buyer* will not perceive it as unfriendly but see it as the *Seller* trying to fully understand the situation. Sometimes, the Seller needs to pull out the big gun to do so. The *Hypothetical Solution* is the big gun.

Caution: When the *Seller* calls the *Buyer* to the carpet it needs to be done in a non-confrontational way. There is the added danger of sounding like a used-car salesman if the *Seller* delivers the *Hypothetical Solution* incorrectly.

Let us walk through the example again and include the *Hypothetical Solution*:

Buyer – "I don't have the funds to allocate to this project."

Seller – "I hear you (*Acknowledge*), it's important to invest your money wisely (*Re-state*)."

Seller – "What is it about the cost that bothers you?" (*Clarify*)

Buyer – " I just don't have the funds, that's all".

Seller – " So if you could afford this you would move ahead right now?" (*Hypothetical Solution*)

Two things to point out; the *Seller* is not promising anything in the solution, merely asking if the objection was not a problem the *Buyer* would buy and then asks for a **commitment** (...move ahead right now?")! It is important to ask for a commitment in the *Hypothetical Solution*.

Second, the *Seller* is phrasing it in such a way as to **not** sound used-car-like. In short what I mean by that is this; "if I get it in red will you buy now?" We have all been subjected to this tactic and it raises our defenses. The way the *Seller* avoids sounding like that is how the *Seller* phrases the question. If the *Seller* ensures the statement is all about the *Buyer* they will not sound sales-like. Read the example again; it is all about the *Buyer*. The words "I", "Me", "Our" or "We" are not in the *Hypothetical Solution*. The words "You" and "Your" are predominant, just like in the rest of the *Decision Process*.

Seller – " So if you could afford this you would move ahead right now?" (*Hypothetical Solution*)

Drilling down further into the psychological aspects of the *Hypothetical Solution*, let us explore what may be going on in the *Buyer's* mind; first, if they are putting up a smokescreen and the Seller delivers a *Hypothetical*

Solution the *Buyer* may be thinking "uh oh, why is she (the *Seller*) asking this? She must have something up her sleeve!" The *Buyer* may also think they have been exposed. This is important and OK because the *Buyer* will now know they cannot pull one over on the *Seller*. We want them to think this. It opens them up to a more reasonable dialogue.

Important: Once the *Hypothetical Solution* is delivered the *Buyer* will do one-of-two things. One is to hesitate or reject the *Hypothetical Solution*. This is a clue that the objection or concern is not real! The other option is to react positive or show interest in the *Hypothetical Solution*, which is a clue the objection or concern is real.

The *Seller* will need to read the reaction and body language of the *Buyer* because the *Buyer's* reaction and clues can be very subtle.

If the *Seller* gathers by the *Buyer's* reaction that the concern or objection is not real they need to do two additional steps.

>Let the *Buyer* know that they obviously have something else that must be bothering them and to please share what it is (more clarification).

>**Once they share another concern the *Seller* must not ever address the first objection. You reject the first objection as if it is not real, therefore you do NOT give it credence.**

I will offer up several more examples of the entire *ARCH* process from start to finish so you can see how it all unfolds. Before I do that let me show you a diagram that explains the flow of the *ARCH* methodology. You may

120

want to copy the diagram and keep in handy for review until you are comfortable with the process. This is not easy to follow at first but it is crucial to dramatically increasing your closing ratio. The real money is made by successfully helping *Buyers* through *Conflict Resolution*.

When the *Buyer* gives the *Seller* an objection, first thing the *Seller* does is implement the *ARCH* methodology below:

> **Acknowledge** – *Seller* acknowledges he heard the *Buyers* concern
>
> > "I hear what you are saying"
>
> **Re-state** – *Seller* re-states the *Buyer's* concern in a manageable way
>
> > "It is important to invest your money wisely"
>
> **Clarify** – Have the *Buyer* clarify their concern
>
> > "What is it about the cost that bothers you?"
>
> **Hypothetical Solution** – *Seller* hypothetically solves and asks for commitment
>
> > "If you had the funds you would go ahead and buy now"?

Refer the matrix boxes below for further clarification of the flow:

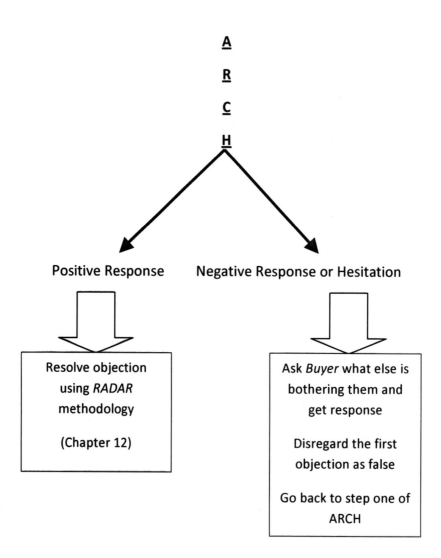

Positive Response	Negative Response or Hesitation
Resolve objection using *RADAR* methodology (Chapter 12)	Ask *Buyer* what else is bothering them and get response Disregard the first objection as false Go back to step one of ARCH

You may need to run several objections through the *ARCH* methodology before getting to the heart of the real issue with the *Buyer*. This is normal and acceptable. At the end of Chapter 12, I will show you what to do if it gets to the point of being ridiculous and the *Buyer* keeps throwing a plethora of new objections at you. *Buyers* who have a real problem with *Fear* may give you the run-around. We have a solution.

Here are several examples of a *Seller* and *Buyer* going through different *ARCH* scenarios from start to finish after the *Seller* asked for the decision. Keep in mind the *ARCH* methodology only takes seconds to a minute, if done correctly. It is a conversation the *Seller* has with the *Buyer* before objections can be fully resolved. We will assume in these examples the *Buyer* has hidden objections.

Scenario # 1: The *Seller* is asking the *Buyer* to purchase a new commercial printer.

Seller – "How does it sound so far?" (asking for decision)

Buyer – "Sounds too expensive, we don't have it in the budget"

Seller – "I can certainly appreciate your concern (*Acknowledge*). It is important to invest your limited budget dollars wisely (*Re-state*). What is it about the price that concerns you?" (*Clarify the objection*)

Buyer – "We just went through a major re-model and don't have the dollars allocated for a new printer."

Seller – "So if you had the money you would purchase the printer today?" (*Hypothetical Solution*)

Buyer – "I didn't necessarily say that." (hesitation, after being backed into a corner)

Seller – "Obviously there is something else going on here, would you mind sharing what it is?"

Buyer - "Well, I am up for a big promotion and if I make a bad decision I won't get the new position".

Seller – "Oh, so it is more about making a good decision, right?" (Disregard the first objection).

Buyer – "Yep, I can't afford to screw this up!"

(*Seller* takes the new objection back to step one)

Seller – "I hear you (*Acknowledge*), it is critical to everyone that you make the right decision (*Re-state*). What about this decision concerns you?"(Clarify)

Buyer – "Well, I made a huge error last time I bought an expensive piece of equipment and my boss nearly tore my head off!"

Seller – "If you could be comfortable your boss would love this decision would that make the difference in moving ahead today?" (*Hypothetical Solution*)

Buyer – "Yes, if I know my boss would love the printer I would feel much better"

This is the real objection, so the *Seller* may now move the RADAR and resolve.

Scenario # 2: The Seller (father) is asking the Buyer (son) to improve grades to avoid summer school.

Seller – "Are you ready to commit to the program to improve your grades?" (asking for decision)

Buyer – "I don't like the schedule. It's too strict!"

Seller – "I can certainly appreciate your concern (*Acknowledge*). It is important to be comfortable that you can accomplish the goal (*Re-state*). What is it about the schedule that bothers you?" (*Clarify the objection*)

Buyer – "It means I will be working on this program for 3 hours a day. That's too much time!"

Seller – "If it were less than three hours a day would you commit to the program?" (*Hypothetical Solution*)

Buyer – "Well... I'm not really sure dad." (hesitation, after being backed into a corner)

Seller – "What else is it son? This isn't that bad of a deal."

Buyer - "Well, I don't think I will ever get algebra, no matter how much time I spend. It's a waste!".

Seller – "So your concerned about the fact that you might be wasting time trying to get through algebra, right?" (Disregard the first objection, do not address!).

Buyer – "Yep, I just don't want to spend all that time and still fail. "

(*Seller* takes the new objection back to step one)

Seller – "I hear you (*Acknowledge*), it is critical that you spend the time knowing you will succeed (*Re-state*). What about algebra concerns you?"(Clarify)

Buyer – "Well, the basic problem is I just don't see how it's relevant so I can't keep focused on it."

Seller – "If you could see where it applies in many areas of real life would that change your mind about committing to the program?" (*Hypothetical Solution*)

Buyer – "Yes, if you can show me that I'd have a different attitude."

This is the real objection, so the *Seller* may now move the RADAR and resolve.

Scenario # 3: The Seller (employee) is asking the Buyer (manager) for a raise.

Seller – "So is 10% reasonable for my merit increase?" (asking for decision)

Buyer – "Believe me I would love to but we are tight on raises this year!"

Seller – "I hear you (*Acknowledge*). You need to do what makes the most sense for the company (*Re-state*). What is it about the 10% that bothers you?" (*Clarify the objection*)

Buyer – "Other employees will all want more. If I do it for you I will need to do it for everybody."

Seller – "If you knew you didn't need to do it for everyone would you be willing to move on this today?" (*Hypothetical Solution*)

Buyer – "Well I am not sure that is feasible." (hesitation, after being backed into a corner)

Seller – "It seems like you are holding something back. Would you mind sharing?"

Buyer - "I don't really see how your performance the past year really merits a 10% raise."

Seller – "So your concern is more about my performance not matching the increase in your mind, right?" **(Disregard the first objection).**

Buyer – " Correct, I just don't know if it makes sense . "

(*Seller* takes the new objection back to step one)

Seller – "I understand your concern (*Acknowledge*), It is important to validate the decision to reward a deserving employee (*Re-state*). What about my performance is in question?"(Clarify)

Buyer – "Well, you only rated average on three of the ten key areas in the merit rating."

Seller – "If there was more clarity around those ratings would that help you to move forward with a better rating and raise?" (*Hypothetical Solution*)

Buyer – "Yes, if you can provide more support for what you accomplished in those areas that might make all the difference."

This is the real objection, so the *Seller* may now move the *RADAR* and resolve.

By reading through these examples (By the way, all real-life examples from graduates of my training program) you get a feel for the flow of *ARCH*. It is just a conversation with the *Buyer* with immense impact on the potential outcome of the *Decision Process*.

Now is the time to add ARCH to our role-play scenario:

Exploration

Seller: Thank you for the information about what is going on here at Acme Roofing. Being a dynamic company you must always be looking out to prevent customer service nightmares. (*SOGI* and official start to the *Buy-Sell-Encounter*)

I mention preventing nightmares because we've been able to do that for many clients. We'd like to do the same for you. (Gap statement before Menu)

You can experience three major benefits with the XR600 system. They are:

Saving money

Preventing unhappy clients due to lost calls

Save time through easy to operate systems

You may get all three, but if you had to select the most important, which would you make number one (have *Buyer* select Menu item)?

Buyer: I would have to say 'preventing unhappy clients'.

Seller: You seem to jump right on that one! What happened? (Intro into the *Journey* and directing the *Buyer* towards the *Pit of Hell*)

Buyer: Well, we just need to keep our clients happier.

Seller: Happier? What do you mean?

Buyer: In today's economic climate we need to hold on to all the customers we can.

Seller: What happens if you don't?

Buyer: Well, lost revenue. Lost revenue means laying crews off.

Seller: What impact will that have on the office?

Buyer: A huge blow to morale.

Selling: What happens then?

Buyer: I may be out of a job (*Pit of Hell*)!

Seller: Ouch, let's try to stop that! Switch it around, what if you had happier clients, what would that change (directing the *Buyer* to *Nirvana*)?

Buyer: Well, we might be able to hire more crews.

Seller: How does that change the game here?

Buyer: More crews means more money for everyone.

Seller: What does that do for you personally?

Buyer: More money means I can retire early and spend time with the grandkids (Nirvana).

Seller: That is a wonderful plan. Thanks for sharing. I have good news; you can make your clients happier with less missed calls, which can keep you from not only losing your job but help you on your way to early retirement (Commitment Statement). Let's see how you can do that.

Validation

Seller: The XR600 has a 99.7% uptime rating from Consumer magazine (*Fact*), making it the highest ranking system of its kind. This means you won't have as many dropped calls and unhappy customers which you said will help protect your job (*Benefit*)!

Next the XR600 allows your staff to see who is calling by name (*Fact*). When they answer the phone and know the name the client has a better disposition about your company. A better disposition means more business, more money and early retirement (*Benefit*)!

Let me show you our "No loss guarantee". If our system doesn't exceed your expectations in the first 30 days we'll re-install your old system at our expense and give you a full refund. (*Defense Diffusion*)

How does it all sound so far (Closing question)?

Buyer: Interesting but we don't have money for capital expenses right now.

Conflict Resolution

Seller: I appreciate that (*Acknowledge*). It is important to invest money wisely in this market (*Re-State the Objection*). What is it about the price that has you concerned (*Clarify*)?

Buyer: We have to watch every penny right now.

Seller: If you had the money or a plan to make it work would you buy the XR600- system today (*Hypothetical Solution*)?

Buyer: Well…I didn't say that…"

Seller: There is obviously something else bothering you. Would you mind sharing what it is?

Buyer: My brother-in-law sold us the last system. He might lose money if we change.

Seller: So it's not so much the price as it is potentially costing your brother-in-law some money, right (disregard the first objection)?

Buyer: Yep. That is a concern.

Seller: I hear you (*Acknowledge*), it is important to make the right people happy (*Re-State*).What is it about him losing money bothers you (*Clarify*)?

Buyer: Well, we have 60 days left on his contract. I don't want problems when we see each other on the weekends.

Seller: If you could wait 60 days to switch, would you commit now?

Once the *Seller* is comfortable knowing the real objection they move to the *Resolution* part of *Conflict Resolution*!

Chapter 12

RADAR

Purpose of *RADAR* - In chapter four we explained there are only four objections: time, money, lack of need/want/desire and *Fear of Change*. We have developed the *Decision Process* all the way to the last stop. Up to now the *Seller* raised the *Level of Interest* in the *Exploration* phase to the highest level with a four-step process, creating a strong emotional bond called the *Buyer's Bond*. The *Buyer* left the *Exploration* phase ready and conditioned to buy and buy now.

The *Seller* then successfully navigated the *Buyer* through *Validation*, proving the product, service or idea to be valid and a good decision for the *Buyer*. The *Seller* finished *Validation* by bringing the *Buyer's* defenses as low as possible and then asked for the decision. The *Sellers* asks for the decision knowing they are heading into *Conflict Resolution*.

In *Conflict Resolution* the patient *Seller* invested time finding the real objection, not "chasing ghosts". The *Seller* knows that *Buyers* sometimes mislead because they might be experience hesitation and *Fear of Change*. After finding the real objection the *Seller* must now find the best possible way to resolve the issue and win the decision for the benefit of the *Buyer* and *Seller*.

RADAR is an acronym for the five powerful methods for resolving conflict and overcome the objection.

Position in the *Decision Process*:

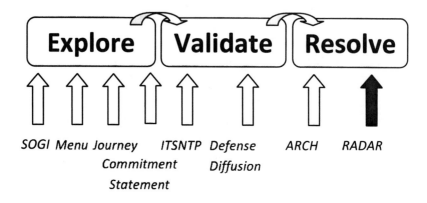

If I have not stressed it enough let allow me to do so one last time; find the real objection first before you try to resolve or overcome. I am saying this to myself as much as I am to anyone reading this book. I get over-excited when a *Buyer* throws out an objection that I know I can resolve easily. The lesson I have had to learn over and over is it does not matter how easy the *Seller* thinks the objection is to overcome, if it is not real the *Seller* will never get there! Lecture over.

The program outlined in this workbook allows a *Seller* to use these *Power Tools* in a moments notice and in almost any situation where a decision is needed. That being said there are certain things of which you want to do your homework. For example, building your *Menu* requires some work, even in an informal setting. You still need to take a moment to craft your *Menu*. From there you need to build your *Menu Matrix* to ensure you have the proper facts, proof and evidence to support your *Menu*. The more you practice the better and faster you become at this valuable skill.

Conflict Resolution is another area whereby we can do planning prior to a *Buy-Sell-Encounter*. You can take time to develop the possible objections to your idea prior to a *Buyer* expressing them. This will greatly boost your confidence before beginning the *Buy-Sell-Encounter*.

This chapter will include a detailed matrix of which *RADAR* methodology to use based on the objection and when to use it. Remember, the actual response needs to come from you. For your formal presentation where you are selling a product or service it a very valuable use of your time to prepare responses to potential conflict and practice the delivery so you sound natural.

Since we know there are only four objections we can also feel comfortable knowing there are only so many responses a *Buyer* can have to disagree or object to our product, service or idea. Do not get overwhelmed, stand back and look at the possibilities of what can go wrong. They are finite and in most cases solvable.

Once we believe we have a good handle on dealing with the real objection and believe it fits into one-of-four categories there is another level of depth we need to breakdown. All objections have two levels: manageable and hopeless. If an objection is truly hopeless we need to walk away to avoid manipulation. You will know it is hopeless as it is usually is very obvious. A good example may be when you are selling a high-ticket item and the business just filed chapter 7. They cannot make any capital purchases, therefore the situation is hopeless.

An objection does not need to be hopeless for the *Seller* to lose the decision. The *Buyer* may have the money, need and want for a product, service or idea but the value is not

established high enough to overcome the cost.
Developing the skills outlined in this book will help move
more "no's" over to the "yes" column. A few more each
week makes a huge difference in our life over a long
period of time.

Let us now dig into the *RADAR* methodology. *RADAR* is
what I call an intelligent acronym, meaning it is spelled the
same forward and backward. It is not something the *Seller*
uses in any order. You may use one, two, three, four or all
five of the methods on one-single objection. What is
important to know is when to use what method. I have
prepared a nice tool towards the end of the chapter to
help guide you but will give the details now.

RADAR represents the five methods to resolve an
objection using the following words:

<u>Re</u>-submit *Proof & Evidence*

<u>A</u>dmission & Silence

<u>D</u>enial & Silence

<u>A</u>sk for Clarification

<u>Re</u>-gift the Objection

Let us break them down one-at-a-time.

<u>Re-Submit Proof & Evidence</u>

Sellers often mistake inquiries or questions as objections
because the *Seller's* defenses are high if the *Buyer* does
not immediately say yes to the decision.

When the *Buyer* asks a question such as "Why is the price so high?" or "How can I possibly find the time?" the *Seller* perceives these as objections. Left alone they can certainly hinder the *Seller's* chances of getting a favorable decision.

There is a known philosophy in the sales world that **all questions, no matter how negative they appear are buying signals**. I subscribe to this philosophy. I will go one step further and add that all objections are buying signals and opportunities for the *Seller* with the right attitude and skill sets.

When a *Buyer* is asking questions with a negative tone the question most likely stems from a lack of understanding about the *Seller's* product, service or idea. If we are confronted with a question with a negative tone we should treat it like any other question; by *Re-Submitting Proof & Evidence*.

***Re-Submit Proof & Evidence* when the objection appears to be a lack of understanding about the *Seller's* solution**. We believe in being laconic when making our presentation in *Validation*. Sometimes in our effort to keep it brief and to-the-point we may have missed a key area. Not a problem as the *Seller* can always back-fill more information as needed. I would rather go back and clarify or add to our evidence rather than talk too much and never get the *Buyer* out of *Validation* before they pull the plug. **This is called talking yourself out of the sale**. We have all experienced this pain before, both as a *Seller* and a *Buyer*.

So, if a *Buyer* asks questions we provide answers. The answers we provide need to follow the guidelines of

Validation. We need to provide *Facts*, not *Claims* and ensure we support the *Facts* with sufficient *Proof & Evidence*.

Summary – The first method for overcoming objections is through powerful *Re-Submission of Proof & Evidence*. After the *Seller Re-Submits Proof & Evidence* she asks closing questions and expects to have more conflict to overcome.

Admission & Silence

The second method for overcoming objections is *Admission & Silence*. In chapter four we discussed the power of silence. Now we can experience the power with this method which has incredible impact to the *Buyer* and *Seller*.

Buyers often think out loud when they are in *Conflict Resolution*. Remember there is a certain amount of turmoil. The *Buyer* is most likely out of their comfort zone and as a result not at their peak. This may cause them to make **confrontational statements** about the *Seller,* product, service or idea. In the last chapter we outlined rules of engagement for dealing with *Conflict Resolution*. One rule is never argue with the *Buyer*. **If the *Buyer* then makes an argumentative statement that is true about the *Sellers'* product, service or idea the *Seller* must be careful not to engage and be defensive.** The *Seller* must show true power, confidence and leadership.

Taking that philosophy to the methodology, if the *Buyer* makes a confrontational remark about the *Sellers'* product, service or idea that is true, the ***Seller* simply admits it is**

true and then goes completely silent. Here a some examples:

Example 1

Buyer – "Yeah, but you've only been in business less than year!"
Seller – "Yep."

Example 2

Buyer – "This product is $3,000 dollars!"
Seller – "Yep".

Example 3

Buyer – "But it takes three weeks to arrive!"
Seller – "Yep."

Now, the crucial next step after the *Seller* admits the *Buyer* is right and goes **silent; the next person to talk "loses".** The *Seller* needs to let the *Buyer* either talk themselves into the decision or ask for more information or clarification.

The *Seller* should not have to defend the truth. If the Seller does, the Seller will sound defensive and weaken their position.

Summary – The second method for overcoming objections is through the power of *Admission & Silence.* Use this method when the *Buyer* makes an **argumentative statement that is true about the *Seller*, product, service or idea.** After the *Seller* admits and goes silent they remain silent until the *Buyer* re-engages. The first one to talk "loses". The *Buyer* may talk themselves into the decision or ask the *Seller* for clarification. Either way the *Seller* has moved the ball forward **without** a confrontation.

Denial & Silence

If *Admission & Silence* is a powerful method then so is *Denial & Silence*. It works in a similar way except the *Seller* will use this when the *Buyer* makes a **baseless, argumentative statement that is not true about the product, service of idea**. When the *Buyer* makes a baseless *Claim* against the *Seller's* product, service or idea the *Seller* still must show great restraint and not correct the *Buyer* or defend the *Claim*.

Example 1

Buyer – "I heard you are going out of business!"
Seller – "Not true."

Example 2

Buyer – "This is just another pyramid scheme!"
Seller – "Not true."

Example 3

Buyer – "You're just like all salespeople; a bunch or liars!"
Seller – "Not true."

Again, there is great power when the *Seller* does not engage in this type of behavior. The *Seller* elevates above the fray and becomes a force to be reckoned with. The same basic rule applies here, after the silence the first one to talk "loses".

If the *Buyer* is looking for a fight or argument they are talking to the wrong person. What often happens after the *Buyer* makes these outrageous remarks and the *Seller* does not engage is the *Buyer* begins to feel silly or even a little guilty and immediately changes their tone. This puts the *Seller* back in control and in the power position.

Summary – The third method for overcoming objections is *Denial & Silence*. The *Seller* uses this method when the *Buyer* makes a baseless, argumentative statement that is not true about the *Seller*, product, service or idea.

Ask for Clarification

In *Conflict Resolution* the *Buyer* by definition is in a state of chaos, regardless of how minor. When in this state the *Buyer* sometimes says things that just don't make any sense. When the *Buyer* is not making sense the Seller needs to ask for clarification. If the *Seller* does not understand fully what the *Buyer's* problem may be and attempts to solve the problem there is a danger of over-selling and further confusing the *Buyer*.

There is nothing wrong with asking for clarification when the *Seller* is confused by the objection. The most common reason for not following this simple method is pride. *Sellers* hate to admit that they do not know something. Another reason is a strong desire not to embarrass the *Buyer*. Although it may seem noble, it serves no purpose at this specific moment.

After the *Seller* asks for clarification they may then choose another method for overcoming the objection. Keep in mind when you *Ask for Clarification* you are talking about the *Buyer*. Wanting to fully understand their concern should not be offensive to the *Buyer* but rather should take it as deep concern for their needs or wants.

Summary – The fourth method of overcoming objections is *Ask for Clarification*. The *Seller* uses this method when the *Buyer* is not making sense.

Re-Gift the Objection

The first four methods are very easy to implement once you embrace the methods. The fifth method is a little different. This is my favorite method. On the surface it seems outrageous and absurd. Then you start to see how it makes 100% sense.

There is nothing wrong with having a little fun and lighten the serious tone of *Conflict Resolution*. This method has that effect if done correctly.

The premise of this method is based on the "shock and awe" theory. The *Seller* may *use* this technique to re-engage the *Buyer* and perhaps keep an otherwise dead *Buy-Sell-Encounter* alive for one more round.

Although I position this method as a "last resort" it really has much more practical application in the mainstream of *Conflict Resolution* when fully understood. The *Sellers* job in the *Buy-Sell-Encounter* is to maintain a high *Level of Interest* throughout the *Decision Process*. It becomes more difficult the further the *Seller* moves the *Buyer* along in the process. The *Re-Gift* method has the ability to snap the *Buyer* back to a high *Level of Interest* quickly (key point: if used properly).

Let us launch into the method. Often the reason the *Buyer* does not make the favorable decision (their objection) is the exact reason why they really need the *Seller's* product, service or idea. Read the previous sentence again. The fact that the *Buyer* may not have the money is exactly why the solution offered by the *Seller* makes sense. The reason the Buyer does not have the time for the product service or idea is the exact reason they need the product, service or idea.

Re-Gift the Objection means to put the objection right back on the *Buyer* as the reason they need the *Seller's* solution!

Examples:

Seller: "The reason you hate salespeople is the exact reason you need to work with me."

Seller: "The fact you have no money is why you need sales training even more!"

Seller: "Your inability to make the decision now is why you need to make the decision now!"

These answers may seem fun and somewhat sensational but here is another point; they all are real and they all worked to move a *Buyer* to a "yes" from a "no"! I know because these are examples I used to get people over the fear of taking my program after they were adamant they would not do it.

When you examine the last few "no's" you may have received in previous *Buy-Sell-Encounters* take a few moments to analyze the situations. **Could the objection the *Buyer* gave be solved if they had bought your solution or agreed with your idea?** You would probably be surprised at how often the *Seller* lets the *Buyer* go when the solution would have solved the objection that the *Seller* bought. As mentioned many times before we are never going to be 100%, we just want to increase the favorable decisions and constantly improve our skills. Again, I am speaking about myself as much as anyone reading this book!

You can use the *Re-Gift* as a last resort or as an opener to an objection. It works in either situation. If the *Seller* wants to lighten the mood they may *start Conflict Resolution* by throwing out a *Re-Gift*. If the mood is more serious the *Seller* may use it at the end to re-engage the *Buyer*. It works in both situations but only the *Buyer* and *Seller* will know when to interject this powerful method. Refer back in chapter 7 when I used the surfing analogy. You as a seller need to feel it.

Summary – Use the *Re-Gift* whenever the *Seller* needs to re-engage the *Buyer* and regain the *Buyer's* full attention. It will invoke a response; sometimes favorable sometimes not but the *Seller* is using the *Re-Gift* because she has nothing to lose at this point. It is better to stay in the game a little longer and perhaps the tide will change. *Sellers* tend to give up too soon on the favorable decision, mostly due to a lack of confidence and understanding while in *Conflict Resolution*.

Always remember to ask closing questions after you apply a methodology! You must re-test the water to see if they are ready to move forward.

Here is the *Objection Matrix.* Copy it and use it until you are comfortable without it.

What To Do	When To Do It
<u>R</u>e-Submit Proof & Evidence	When the *Buyer* is asking questions
<u>A</u>dmission & Silence	When the *Buyer* makes an argumentative statement that is true about the *Seller,* product, service or idea
<u>D</u>enial & Silence	When the *Buyer* makes an argumentative statement that is false about the *Seller,* product, service or idea
<u>A</u>sk for Clarification	When the *Buyer* isn't clear or making sense. Do not guess!
<u>R</u>e-Gift the Objection	Whenever we need to re-engage the *Buyer* and grab their attention

Chapter 13

Practical Application

Now it is time to illustrate an example of taking a *Buyer* through the entire *Buy-Sell-Encounter* process so you may see how the process flows. This will conclude the role-play scenario we have developed throughout the book, adding a new *Power Tool* with each new chapter.

Understand, that to be truly influential you need to be so all of the time, not just when asking for a *Buyer* to buy a product or service. We use a sales situation because it is the easiest to illustrate and understand.

Spoiler Alert: The *Seller* wins the decision.

Here is a crucial point that needs to be made. We don't always start at the very beginning of the *Decision Process* i.e. start with a *SOGI*. It is a *Decision Process* (I will never tire of reminding everyone this) not a selling process. The *Buyer* is aware of where they are in the process and the skilled *Seller* knows where the *Buyer* is and can jump in with the *Buyer* at that point and help guide the *Buyer* to a successful conclusion.

For example if a *Buyer* says to a *Seller* "My friend uses your product and said I really need it. How does it work?" This *Buyer* already has a high *Level of Interest*, meaning they have likely done the *Journey* in their head prior to your meeting. They are asking questions meaning they likely are in *Validation*. It would look canned and contrived if you as the *Seller* started with a *SOGI*.

If a *Buyer* starts the *Buy-Sell-Encounter* saying "My friend loves your service but I don't think I can afford it" a skilled *Seller* would recognize the *Buyer* is in *Conflict Resolution*.

You understand. The key is to develop a keen sense of where the *Buyer* already is in the process and be there with them. A key method to find out is to ask a few simple questions. These questions may sound like closing questions. It is a great way to gauge the *Buyer's* location in the *Decision Process*.

Let us now show the entire the *Buy-Sell-Encounter*:

As a reminder here is the scenario:

The Seller is a sales professional. Her product is the XR600 phone system. The Buyer is an office manager for a 30 employee roofing business. They set a meeting, had *Casual Conversation* and then the *Seller* qualified the *Buyer* in *Exchange of Information & Direction*.

Exploration

Seller: Thank you for the information about what is going on here at Acme Roofing. Being a dynamic company you must always be looking out to prevent customer service nightmares. (*SOGI* and official start to the *Buy-Sell-Encounter*)

I mention preventing nightmares because we've been able to do that for many clients. We'd like to do the same for you. (Gap statement before Menu)

You can experience three major benefits with the XR600 system. They are:

Saving money

Preventing unhappy clients due to lost calls

Save time through easy to operate systems

You may get all three, but if you had to select the most important, which would you make number one (have *Buyer* select Menu item)?

Buyer: I would have to say 'preventing unhappy clients'.

Seller: You seem to jump right on that one! What happened? (Intro into the *Journey* and directing the *Buyer* towards the *Pit of Hell*)

Buyer: Well, we just need to keep our clients happier.

Seller: Happier? What do you mean?

Buyer: In today's economic climate we need to hold on to all the customers we can.

Seller: What happens if you don't?

Buyer: Well, lost revenue. Lost revenue means laying crews off.

Seller: What impact will that have on the office?

Buyer: A huge blow to morale.

Selling: What happens then?

Buyer: I may be out of a job (*Pit of Hell*)!

Seller: Ouch, let's try to stop that! Switch it around, what if you had happier clients, what would that change (directing the *Buyer* to *Nirvana*)?

Buyer: Well, we might be able to hire more crews.

Seller: How does that change the game here?

Buyer: More crews means more money for everyone.

Seller: What does that do for you personally?

Buyer: More money means I can retire early and spend time with the grandkids (Nirvana).

Seller: That is a wonderful plan. Thanks for sharing. I have good news; you can make your clients happier with less missed calls, which can keep you from not only losing your job but help you on your way to early retirement (Commitment Statement). Let's see how you can do that.

Validation

Seller: The XR600 has a 99.7% uptime rating from Consumer magazine (*Fact*), making it the highest ranking system of its kind. This means you won't have as many dropped calls and unhappy customers which you said will help protect your job (*Benefit*)!

Next the XR600 allows your staff to see who is calling by name (*Fact*). When they answer the phone and know the name the client has a better disposition about your company. A better disposition means more business, more money and early retirement (*Benefit*)!

Let me show you our "No loss guarantee". If our system doesn't exceed your expectations in the first 30 days we'll re-install your old system at our expense and give you a full refund. (*Defense Diffusion*)

How does it all sound so far (Closing question)?

Buyer: Interesting but we don't have money for capital expenses right now.

Conflict Resolution

Seller: I appreciate that (*Acknowledge*). It is important to invest money wisely in this market (*Re-State the Objection*). What is it about the price that has you concerned (*Clarify*)?

Buyer: We have to watch every penny right now.

Seller: If you had the money or a plan to make it work would you buy the XR600 system today (*Hypothetical Solution*)?

Buyer: Well...I didn't say that..."

Seller: There is obviously something else bothering you. Would you mind sharing what it is?

Buyer: My brother-in-law sold us the last system. He might lose money if we change.

Seller: So it's not so much the price as it is potentially costing your brother-in-law some money, right (disregard the first objection)?

Buyer: Yep. That is a concern.

Seller: I hear you (*Acknowledge*), it is important to make the right people happy (*Re-State*).What is it about him losing money bothers you (*Clarify*)?

Buyer: Well, we have 60 days left on his contract. I don't want problems when we see each other on the weekends.

Seller: If you could wait 60 days to switch, would you commit now?

Buyer: I would. Is that possible? (Buyer asks a question, so *Seller* select *Re-Submit Proof & Evidence* to resolve and overcome)

Seller: As a matter of fact we can lock in the price with a small deposit and install the program in 60 days (*Fact*), giving you the comfort of not costing your brother-in-law money (*Benefit*).

How does that sound (closing question)?

Buyer: Much better.

Seller: Shall we go over the paperwork and terms?

Buyer: Sure!

Favorable decision – *Win/Win*

I wish all *Buy-Sell-Encounters* went this well but you get the point. There is a flow to the process.

Summary points to remember:

- ✓ Knowing where the *Buyer* is in the *Decision Process* is as crucial as knowing what to do while in the process.

- ✓ We are in *Buy-Sell-Encounters* all day every day. You need to recognize you are in it and know how to win it. Influence is 24/7.

- ✓ Taking time to prepare before a *Buy-Sell-Encounter* greatly increases the chances of getting a favorable decision.

- ✓ Practice does not make perfect but rather permanent. Ensure you practice the proper way so the methods become skills.

- ✓ Skills diminish. Use them or lose them.

- ✓ **Do not fear objections, embrace them and your confidence and attitude will be evident in the *Buyer's* mind. People want to work with people they know and trust. Leadership and confidence help build trust.**

Off to wrap things up!

Chapter 14

Final Thoughts

I said in chapter four someone can want something forever and never buy it. When they need it they will take action now. The same holds true for what you may do with the information and knowledge you garnered from this book. You need to make your personal development a priority. Everybody wants to, but few make it a priority.

According to the Department of Health & Human Services 99% of Americans by age 65 never achieve wealth. I believe the wealthy are there not as a result of luck or chance. They are entrepreneurs as well as corporate employees. They are professionals and business owners. If you list all the possible characteristics of the wealthy 1% you might say they are risk takers, driven, motivated, focused etc. Want to know a secret? None of those characteristics mean anything towards success. These characteristics do not guarantee one penny will be made.

Do you know the **one** common characteristic all business-savvy wealthy people have? The one thing that guarantees they will always be wealthy? The common thread they all share is this; they are the best salespeople in their chosen fields. The wealthy 1% are truly the most influential people in the world.

We are sometimes so ashamed of sales in this country we need to disguise the name. Know this; selling is the highest paying job in the world.

We are taught in America that if you want security you need to give up freedoms and work for a company as an employee. If you want freedom you can quit that job, start your own business but lose security. The only profession which allows for both incredible security and incredible freedom is sales. Embrace it and be proud!

About the Author

Don Spini has been in sales, sales management and senior-level sales executive positions for major corporations for 25 years. In those 25 years he has been through virtually every sales training program available. It was all valuable but was missing key components.

In 1995 at the age of 32 Don set a goal to retire before age 50 and to do so using his own sales & influence methodology he created and detailed in this book.

Don hit his goal four years early. Wanting to share this program with others Don launched his own sales training company in 2009.

Today Don's company, PRO Force has locations in several US markets offering high-level training to individuals and corporations. His premier workshop, Sixty-Seconds to Yes has helped professionals from all walks of life sell more and live more fulfilling lives as leaders through advanced communication skills. Don personally conducts over 150 training sessions a year, making him the most prolific and top sales trainer in the nation.

Don is a keynote speaker for major conventions and corporate events. Don's real passion is being with his wife and children and working on his ranch in San Diego, CA.

CPSIA information can be obtained at www.ICGtesting.com
Printed in the USA
LVOW07*0527060615

441323LV00001B/10/P